A Field Guide to Losing Your Friends

A FIELD GUIDE TO LOSING YOUR FRIENDS

Essays on Loss

+

BY TYLER DUNNING

Riverfeet
Press

One essay in this collection has appeared elsewhere:

"Brother of Eagle" in *Dogwood: A Journal of Poetry and Prose*

Published by
Riverfeet Press
riverfeetpress.com

ISBN 978-0-692-87229-1
LCCN 2017937757

This is a work of non-fiction though the names of certain individuals have been changed.

Cover design by Steve Witmer
Book design by Tyler Dunning & Steve Witmer

For Nate, Shane, John, Janice, and Terry.

+

CONTENTS

+

We Are All Trees
Introduction

———————

I take great interest in trees—interest, more specifically, in the details that go unnoticed. Aspen trees, for example, look an innocent and mundane enough timber—except, of course, in their fall foliage—but beneath the surface, quite literally, a different story is being told. Aspen trees have a communal root system: water and nutrients extracted from the soil are shared holistically by the grove. This is why, in the fall, each tree changes hue in unison with the brothers and sisters surrounding it—a series of seemingly independent trees rising together.

As another example, Joshua trees, when uninhibited, grow in pillar shapes. It's when a Joshua tree freezes that a blossom can occur, and when a Joshua tree blossoms, it causes the tree to split and grow in two separate directions.

Trunks that support numerous branches have likely frozen and blossomed just as many times. This, to the bewildered observer, is a sight often unrecognized as the result of shock and discomfort, growth and change.

And finally, redwoods are among the most diligent trees on the planet: insects do not weaken them; fungus does not infect them; fire rarely kills them. They are gods among saplings, the monarchs of the forest. But, although strong and mighty, they are nurturing. Redwoods bring life to the whole forest—from the tiny clover to the formidable fir. And when a redwood does finally fall, it is not uncommon for multiple other trees to grow out of its corpse and live off the lasting legacy now dissolving back in to the dirt.

There is much to learn from our arbor kindred, the list extensive—but this is not a book about biology or ecology, nor is this a book endorsing the hugging of dendrites or advocating the protection of the planet. This is a coming-of-age collection of non-chronological essays depicting my struggle through the simple act of being alive, coexisting, and growing out of a common chaos—memoir in staccato, if you will. These essays are the metaphorical love letters I never sent to all the complex facets of life that often go unnoticed and remain underappreciated—root systems, growth patterns, necessary decay. But I'm sending them now.

I'm sending them in the realization that this book is precisely about autobiographical biology, esoteric ecology, and protecting all that sustains our storytelling: bark, feather, and fur. Because we are all trees. And, like a hard freeze before a beautiful blossom, we need communal stories to branch out beyond our uniform comfort zones; we need communal stories to rise like future kings and queens from the royalty that reared us.

So, taking stock in the therapeutic power of prose, consider this an invitation to share these very roots . . . and grow with me.

+

THE GEOLOGY OF
HARD LOSS

"Natural processes can cause hazardous conditions at any time, even in 'safe' areas where no incidents have been observed previously."

—The National Park Service

✝

Lush and Alive
Estes Park, Colorado

———————

On July 11, 2010 a series of explosions erupted across Kampala, Uganda—terrorist attacks orchestrated by a Somali militant group looking to raise a little hell: one bomb gutted an Ethiopian restaurant while another tore across a rugby field where the men's FIFA World Cup championship match was being shown. Seventy-four innocent people were murdered that evening.

Some died more immediately than others. Some fought, choked, hacked to stay alive. Some lay sprawled across plastic lawn chairs, overturned and broken, with white linen clothing blotched crimson from the inside out. Other bodies littered the grass, survivors screaming to the disarray.

Several were rushed to the hospital in a fleeting hope.

One of them was Nate Henn, the muzungu, the white man who now had a little shrapnel in his chest. *I can't breathe*, he kept saying. *I can't breathe*. His last words. Last breath. My best friend.

By the end of that summer, seventy-two days after the bombings, I found myself alone on the wrong side of Longs Peak. I'd been told the hike was going to be dangerous, that people died on that mountain every year. In fact, a man had just fallen to his death weeks earlier. But despite the warnings, there I was, advancing along a thousand-foot cliff face in northern Colorado.

The trek was wishful thinking: internal struggle made tangible, a high-altitude hike exchanging mental torment for the palpability of physical pain. I was there to sweat my sufferings; to seep all haunting memory from my mind. There because I wanted to believe solace was a wild thing best fostered in a forest; that many tormented souls, all coming before me, had found refuge just the same. There, having chosen Longs, because I wanted to believe if I could get over that mountain maybe—just maybe—I could get over my loss.

So I went where people die—hoping to feel alive—only to find the route too sheer for hiking. I was seeking an opening referred to as "the Keyhole" that, once through, would lead me to the pinnacle of Longs, the highest point in the park—14,259 feet—the keeper of the rocky crown.

I scrambled from one boulder to the next, and with each massive rock—rocks the size of Volkswagens—I had to catch my breath, the air thinning and proving a hardy chore to my untrained lungs. *I can't breathe*, I kept thinking, *I can't breathe*. Then I thought about shrapnel. And punctured lungs. I thought about what it really means not to breathe—

My plan wasn't working: even with depleted oxygen I couldn't arrest remembrance. I had to focus—

Slower breaths. Deeper breaths. Slower breaths. Deeper breaths—

I kept on, to a vertical crack, and using the minor climbing skills I'd learned over the course of the now-ending summer—hand over hand, foot above foot, higher and higher—I kept on. This would have been fine had I not suffered from a debilitating fear of heights, but such circumstances were offering little leeway. Only when I found artificial bolts, for technical rope climbing, jutting from the rock did I realize, without a doubt, I'd made a mistake. I was on the wrong path.

I stabilized on a nook-like ledge and scanned the landscape below, a panoramic view giving clear sight of the actual Keyhole—the broken arch acting as a rite of passage on the exact *opposite* side of the remaining mountain. Anxiety ensued as dread coerced my body into a psychosomatic battle—by thinking about falling my organs would recoil, sending flu-like symptoms to my joints, stomach, and lungs. I thought I was going to fall to a quick and harrowing boulder-dashed death, blood and brains strewn on the rocks below. I thought I was going to die.

The first time I saw it, summer was in full swing yet snow still somehow graced the mountain cathedrals around me. A local man pointed toward the heavens: *That one*, he said, *with the notch missing. It's that one.*

Longs, like an untouchable icon. An itch. An obsession.

I knew I had to conquer it, the unassuming mountain amongst the many. This was still two months before my attempt—two months of admiring from below.

I was there, in Estes Park, Colorado, to work at the Della Terra Mountain Chateau, where ornate weddings commenced nearly every night. It was a seasonal position adding yet another link to my chain of temporary endeavors—a lifestyle conditioning me to believe six months was *far too long* to settle in any one place. This was Colorado via Montana via California via Florida via Israel via California via Western Europe via Montana via Missouri via Montana. I enjoyed the travel, but it became a form of self-torture: every *via* fueled by some newly discovered form of neurosis—bad brain, as my dear old brother calls it.

Every *via* made me think of birds. Migration. A calling to move wired so deep in our psyches that we often don't even know why we do it. Across plains, ecotones, flyways. Across continents and oceans. Sometimes never landing. Periodic, large-scale movement. Periodic, and repeated.

Some birds, like my older brother, are permanent residents and do not migrate. They have secured adequate resources, even in trying times. They've found meaning, or maybe, just don't fixate on it. Some go short- to mid-range distances, like a grandparent who winters away in, say, Arizona. They're happy, either here or there. Near or far. But others undertake arduous journeys—long-distance flight. They don't know when to stop.

I kept flying because I had no anchor points—no girl, no career, no kids—and after drifting this way for a decade, being in the latter half of my twenties, I was feeling less a loser and more a failure. Somehow all my small victories had added up to one grand disappointment. Maybe I was migrating for the wrong reasons. Maybe I'd kept moving if only to keep from killing myself.

During this period a fellow vagabond invited me to work at her family's chateau, an enchanting castle buried deep in the heart of the Rocky Mountains, and I was intrigued: I could yet again postpone any major life decisions, at least for another season. It would allow me to live in Estes with five close friends while being only minutes from Rocky Mountain National Park. I couldn't wait to begin.

But the job started in a month. I went home to kill time.

Montana is always a slow sojourn, a lazy river of living nostalgia. I first left the state at nineteen to pursue the pipedream of professional wrestling. Then, over the next decade, I came back occasionally, carrying quiet discontent in my heart, never quite forgiving of the place that had done me no harm.

I smoked hookah on Wednesdays, wrote in the evenings, watched obscure television with my mom at night. Childhood friends remained as I'd left them, and we were quick to pick up where we'd left off: video games, weight lifting, downtown drinking. The break was a release from restlessness, the most exciting news concerning matters of soccer: four days before I left for Estes Park, the 2010 FIFA World Cup championship match commenced— Spain vs. the Netherlands. Friends and family joined to watch, digitally connecting to the planet through a shared sense of sportsmanship—the world, as if standing still for the spectacle.

"Who's in the orange again?"

"The Dutch, Mom."

"Do we want them to win?"

"Yeah, *Mom*, Spain can eat dirt."

"Why're you talking like that? You don't even care about sports."

This, of course, was true, proven when Spain won and yet nothing was lost to my heart. As the competitive dust settled—the world set back in motion—my mom and I lingered before the TV, shifting focus to a fantasy thriller in which good vs. evil is demonstrated through a well-choreographed clashing of swords.

"You gonna get that, Tyler?"

"Huh?"

"Your phone."

"Nah."

"I can pause it."

"It's fine."

"That's rude, you know."

"What?"

"Answer your phone, Tyler."

"Mom!"

"What?"

"Watch the show."

But the vibrations kept coming. I opened my texts:

I'm so sorry.

Please let me know if there is anything I can do to help.

Tyler . . . I don't know what to say.

I'm praying for you.

Call me if you need someone to—

"What's wrong?" my mom asked.

"I—I don't, but . . . someone's dead. One of my friends."

"How do you know that? Why are you saying that?" The panic on her face was a mirror to my own.

"I don't know"—a list was forming in my head with only a couple of names standing out, the travelers, Nate making the most sense—"but somebody's dead."

I'd worked with Nate for nearly two years at a non-profit called Invisible Children—an organization dedicated to bringing sustainable peace to war-affected parts of Central East Africa through educational opportunities, economic advancements, and international diplomacy. Nate and I had traveled the United States together—living out of a van for months at a time—giving presentations at high schools, universities, and places of worship to help raise advocacy and awareness. He joined my New England-based team after a different member had resigned. We picked up Nate in transit between presentations, somewhere in Connecticut, his training a trial by fire.

In the hallways of high schools and in the guest rooms of churches, I taught him what he needed to know: the history of the war, the consequences of such violence, and all the humanitarian programs we were helping to promote. He knew the basics, but I gave every nuanced detail of my historical mind: dates, statistics, politics, socioeconomics, international relations. This was the Lord's Resistance Army abducting tens of thousands of kids and forcing them to become child soldiers or sex slaves, this was an auto-genocide against the Acholi people, this was the displacement of entire communities for fear of murder and mutilation. *This* was the apex of crimes against humanity that the world at large was largely ignoring.

The subject matter was heavy, but the downtime with Nate always playful. "Tyler, do that thing where you kick me in the head."

"The pro wrestling thing?"

"Yeah, kick me in the head."

"It's gonna hurt on the concrete."

"I don't care. It'll freak people out. Just do it—"

I flew through the air.

"*Shit!*"

"What?"

"That *really* hurt."

"I told you it was gonna—"

"Hey . . . look." People were staring. People were always looking to Nate.

He left for Uganda after we'd both completed our second tours with Invisible Children (this time on different teams) to visit friends and examine firsthand the groundwork we'd advocated so ardently for across the United States. I was excited to hear of his travels, but more so, for Nate to return home—there was talk of him working at the chateau with us. But Nate *was* at the rugby field with three other friends on that July evening. Of the group, he was the only one physically afflicted by the explosion, catching a piece of shrapnel in his chest, his lungs. *I can't breathe*, he kept saying, *I can't breathe.*

I learned these details after returning a friend's call, the conversation brief but with bullet-point facts: terror, murder, loss. Hanging up, I found myself outside, hunched in the grass. I wanted to throw up. I wanted to throw my phone against the house, full force, the way Nate and I used to throw our Frisbee across New England's far-reaching parks as a means of breaking up monotonous drives. Back and forth, giving and taking, like our late-night conversations in the van regarding religion, favorite bands, and girls. Always girls. (Nate loved girls. Tall girls. Blond girls. Jewish girls. Smart-brained girls. G-chatting girls. Ex girls. New girls. Sassy girls. Hippie girls. Because, more than anything, Nate *loved* girls.)

"I'm telling you, it works every time!" he joked. "All you gotta do is grab the face!" He extended his hand before him, while driving, over the steering wheel toward the windshield, as if cusping the cheek of an imagined woman.

"Bullshit."

"When we get to New York you try it on that girl you've been jammin' on. She'll kiss you. Right on the lips, I swear."

"You're saying all I have to do is this"—I, too, cusped the air.

"That's right, my man."

"*Bull*shit."

"Tyler, he's right," Brit and Anna chimed in from the backseat, two others also traveling with us. "It works."

I turned back to Nate—his hand waiting to grab *my* face. "Admit it," he said, "you *almost* just kissed me!" I leaned in, lips puckered, spiteful, to which he twisted his hand, palmed my face, and pushed me away. We laughed, like a holiday.

Before Nate left, I told him I had a girl story to share but he asked me to wait, wanting something to look forward to upon coming home.

Upon coming home . . .

What a novel idea, getting to come home. And what hollow safety we place in such notions, in the I'll-see-you-laters and the I'll-talk-to-you-soons, because when they never come, and when we're robbed of our taken-for-granted worldviews, it shakes us. And it breaks us. Because I couldn't fathom why it was him, a man who loved being alive, and not someone like me, a man who contemplated suicide daily. Why it was *him*, a man who wanted nothing more than to have a family of his own, a man who dreamt about coaching little league baseball and tormenting any potential suitors his future daughters might have—

I threw my phone against the house and rose like a phoenix, everything exploding into a supernova brighter than a thousand suns. I became, all at once, an infected wound. A human body—as a single cell to the entire species—now cancerous and metastasizing. After all, that's how hate works. How violence spreads.

Back inside, in my mother's arms, the television continued—just residual noise at that point—a program unfolding as planned: swords, magic, bloodshed. But that day there had been another struggle between good and evil, this one un-choreographed and without the story-arced ending designed to make us feel like God, or whatever, was still on our side. And an important part of everything was lost to my heart. Nate was dead.

I left for Colorado dim. A star after collapse. A surge and fade. Bright then dim. I left blighted—a wilting without decay—ten hours of driving and no way of setting my mind to cruise control. I passed the spot where Custer made his last stand. Segued from mountains to foothills to plains. The world, in all its former majesty, seemed blighted with me.

But Wyoming, in the middle of my path, gleamed green. Wyoming was beautiful, something I seldom thought about the neighboring state, everything lush and alive that season. Streams gushed from newly acquired snowmelt—water gifted from the great divide. Golden rolling slopes brimmed with winter wheat ready for harvest, sugar beets ripe for uprooting. The sky clear canvas. The road familiar.

I arrived in Estes Park by night, the depth of blackness pockmarked with stars and a waning moon. Elk and deer stood as phantoms in the car headlights, coming to observe if the rumors were true: another broken soul seeks refuge in the wilderness. I arrived as an infected wound, helpless to any form of healing, with my days so filled with rage I couldn't see straight, my nights so filled with loss I couldn't sleep right. I was in Estes—but I wasn't.

Evenings planned with friends to go bowling or see a movie were eclipsed by solitude at the river or unaccompanied drives into the woods. It was that or whiskey, cigarettes, and silence. I just couldn't shake this strange new paradigm of darkness forced upon me and illuminating the age-old truth that life is only possible with loss, and loss only meaningful through love. But this loss was hardly warranted—with my heart not breaking, but bearing and bearing and bearing and bearing—

I didn't want to believe it. I just wanted my friend back. But instead, I was given ponderosa, aspen, cabins amongst wilderness. Weddings, campgrounds, a chateau. Another new home.

Rocky Mountain National Park nests directly in the backbone of the North American continent, named for the mountain range stretching all the way from Canada to Mexico. Being from Montana, this region didn't feel too far from home—a well-timed comfort.

I relished the century-old history of the park, a designated area set to protect and preserve the radical terrain ranging from montane to alpine, glacier-cut valleys to coniferous forests, towering waterfalls to lush meadows.

I studied the wildlife—the feeding patterns of pikas and the bugle of elk. I spent days observing Albert's squirrels and Steller's jays, chasing wild turkeys out of wedding photos, herding bighorn sheep off the parking lots. And those black bears—clever beasts leaving a path of destruction across hummingbird feeders and park dumpsters.

Rocky Mountain National Park also harbors the northernmost fourteen-thousand-foot mountain in Colorado: Longs Peak. The only way to approach Longs is by hiking; the national park as a whole contains over three-hundred miles of hiking trails. I lived on those trails, weaving in and out of grand peaks, pristine streams, and motionless lakes. Always watching from a distance though, was Longs.

I first visited Rocky Mountain National Park days after arrival, the place still veiled in mystery, taking a spontaneous 2 a.m. drive once that evening's wedding had ended and the chateau glistened to our late-night labor. We drove in darkness, everything invisible as our eyes fought to formulate shapes beyond the headlights. This was Trail Ridge Road, the highest major highway in the U.S., an elevated precipice with endless wilderness at either side. This was an altitude even the forest couldn't reach—trees unable to tolerate such harsh conditions.

Choosing an arbitrary pull-off, we parked the car and trekked across alpine shrub and boulders. We were together, six in total, but solitary in thought. Thanks to the moonlight, we could see the winding rivers, the formidable fir and pine, the reflective lakes created by eighteen thousand years of glacial history. Tears came as if beckoned, undammed only by death, and joined the watershed.

What came next may have been a prayer or cathartic ramble or one and the same. I spoke to Nate—I spoke knowing if he was ever to hear me, it would be in this spot, on this ledge, safe amongst the wild. Protected. It was the last conversation I'd ever have with him.

The funeral came two weeks later. I found myself in Delaware, transfixed before a coffin adorned with photos, flowers, and a Red Sox baseball cap. It's a convolution of memories now, recollection filtered through the blur of sorrow—sadness like snow blanketing the weekend. Or coastal fog. A true tragedy, it is, our body's ability to repress pain. Our rot of remembrance.

The service lasted hours, and yet, little now percolates up through my memory. I remember meeting Nate's parents. I remember learning about Nate's life before I knew him. I remember having to say goodbye to one of the closest brothers I'd ever have. And to think, by this time, Nate should have been home, safe, and working at the chateau with us—not a shell, in a coffin, haunting a world to which he once gave color.

The chateau became many things to us, the summer staff, but first and foremost it was a place of marriage, each afternoon filled with a ceremony down the long stone path near the pond and gazebo. Each reception with the same tired speeches, the same classically catered meals and wine. Each DJ with identical music. Weddings became as reliable as the circadian sun. But there was still magic in the matrimonial mundane: we were giving the visiting hopeful a chance to solidify their luck on a romantic gamble.

But behind the curtains—behind the bells, whistles, and brides—the chateau stood as an undeclared refuge, a place for the lost and transient to observe a love for which they were still looking. And, haphazardly, we were always trying to find it: an attractive caterer or event planner became a fleeting hope for a first date; drunken wedding guests became a way to feel wanted; and fellow employees, unfortunately, became false remedies to a loneliness that only mountain living can induce. There was no beginning, no end, and caught in the middle, we were six: chateau kids with a shared history of heartache. We generated drama and mischief—

Movie nights. Wrestling matches. Headlocks. Maggots coming from the plumbing. Skype nights with ex-girlfriends. Hikes. Visiting friends. Vegetarianism in an elk town. Scouting bears in golf carts. Imagining each other naked. Imagining each other dead. Hookah. Hookah. Hookah. More hikes. YouTube videos. Skinny dipping. Seeing each other naked. Masturbating in the shower. Self-loathing. Bars. Drinkin'. Doin' that good ol' bad brain dance. Karaoke, baby. Dance, dance. Revolution. And we, lost boys and girls of the Peter Pan variety, made even the most mundane work-nights tolerable:

"You know what I worry about more than anything?" Michael asked.

"A raccoon. In the dumpster."

"No. A *bear* in the dumpster," he said, entering the garbage shed.

"That's pretty unlikely," I said, opening the dumpster lid, "the doors are always—" A raccoon popped its head out of the trash, its face a foot from our own.

I turned to run, accidentally swinging a flattened cardboard box against Michael and knocking him into the raccoon, its teeth exposed. I then smashed my own forehead against the half-ajar metal door. Michael stuck the raccoon with an empty wine bottle and fled, only to topple over my prostrate body. We both crawled and squirmed outside in the hopes of safety, as the raccoon, just as debilitated, and horrified, scampered over our bodies, disappearing to freedom. We lay in disbelief, laughing until tears streamed down our faces.

"I . . . can't . . . believe . . ."

"Did . . . that . . . really . . . just . . ." We laughed till our abs hurt. We couldn't breathe—

Then I remembered what it means not to breathe. And guess who was on my mind? Because when someone dies, you keep their number in your phone, because you're afraid to delete it, because what *exactly* does it mean when you do? When someone dies, you re-read every letter or email or text they ever sent—hundreds of times— and now, somehow, the very curve of their penmanship becomes a subtle grace you never recognized before because now it's extinct, gone; you're holding a relic, a bread crumb, a historical document to your former happiness. You can study what it used to feel like, that sweet happiness. But you can't will it back into existence. You can never go back across that thin ripple in time when terrorism was just terrorism. To a time when a bomb was just a bomb, waiting to become brighter than a thousand suns, before it was all shrapnel and punctured lungs and dead friends rotting back to carbon and chemicals in caskets in the earth. Bright then dim. A wilting without decay—

I couldn't breathe. And guess who was on my mind?

Triggers were everywhere. Simply turning on the TV could mess me up, as, for the first couple of weeks, Nate was there too. Even in death everybody looked to him, but this time it really was *everyone*. Nate was the only American killed in the incident and, for unacceptable sociopolitical reason, this gave him substantial prominence over the others murdered. Nate stole the show.

His face graced syndications around the globe. They told his story: twenty-five years old, a product of Delaware and North Carolina, an altruistic peacekeeper. A brother's brother. A mother's son. And let me tell you, it's a *weird fucking thing* losing your best friend to the celebrity of his ghost—having to divvy your wrecking-ball sob story with the rest of the world—yet no one was asking my two cents. I wanted to talk about him. To be closer to him. To remember him. To love him. But silence spiraled into jealousy and selfishness and delusion. Into Shame.

So I'd have another drink. Get drunk. A lot. Alone. Stay that way for longer hours of the day for more days of the week. I wanted Nate back. I wanted *my* Nate back.

I began clinging to any fragment of hope—like shrapnel—that could bring purpose back to my pain. What should have been a summer paradise had become a turbulent test of character. But the more I withdrew, the more I explored. And it was the mountains that pulled me back in and offered me the fundamental truths I needed. Because the more I was learning about nature, the more I was learning about myself. It was my exploration of Rocky Mountain National Park that restored this life in me. And this is what inspired me to make a solo attempt at Longs Peak. This is why reaching the top was so important.

Looking down from my perch, having taken the wrong route up Longs, survival meant backtracking the unpromising crack. A steady gale tore across the terrain, gusts having already knocked me over twice on the voyage up. So I crawled like a cloud down the mountain, clinging to avoid flight, a gut-rot feeling overtaking my body—physical ill-ness generated by mental fear. Vomit crept up my throat when feet slipped from holds, fingers my only anchor. And this is how it went, inch by inch, until I moved closer to safety, and finally, to steady ground.

I faced the Boulder Field again, keeping me from the actual Keyhole—a distance that would take at least anoth-er hour to traverse. I looked to the sky and thought about the approaching afternoon: I'd been warned not to be on Longs' summit after midday due to lightning storms. I thought about this, considered the intense wind, and knew I'd been defeated. It was time to accept my disappoint-ment.

But the descent from Longs didn't come without its own dangers. Coming around an arching bend, losing sight of the path behind me, I was both mystified and terrified to observe a mountain lion on the nearing slope. It stopped about fifty yards from me, sat on the trail, and stared. And as if this great hunter was Medusa herself, I became paralyzed to its eyes. I'd read all the literature: that it's best to look big, make loud noises, and never show fear. But all this information left my mind as I stood there turning to stone. The encounter felt like eternity, but in truth it lasted maybe thirty seconds.

I stood there long after the feline had left, reminded that I could have perished that day, by cliff or claw, but chance took favor on me. Because sometimes hikers *do* fall off cliffs, sometimes humans *are* attacked by wildlife, and sometimes people *choose* to murder each other in the name of terror. Sometimes death is just death. Sometimes it's not. Things just cross our paths.

I'd made my attempt at Longs, failing, and now my time in Colorado was over, autumn already making its presence known—in the air, on the leaves. Soon mulch. Then decay. The wedding season had ended, too, and I'd be moving back to California soon, to work for Invisible Children yet again. My life on a loop. My migratory patterns prolonged.

All the while I kept perpetual motion, still haunted, still searching, and silently hiking across this nation—through the backcountry of my own curiosity and consciousness, always feeling incomplete and never sure if it was because of that mountain, my madness, or mankind. I kept flying, further, hoping there would be another time and place for Longs, maybe when my heart, like the mountain, was more willing to forgive. I kept flying, *further*—writing and rewriting, in my head, the rough draft to all of my damage, a field guide to losing my friends—knowing someday I'd be back to finish that hike.

+

The Bridges of Gallatin County
Cody, Wyoming

———————

Lessons in loss come in many forms. Death, certainly, but just as common is that of romance. Sometimes they coincide. This was my first lesson in both . . .

The relationship had gotten weird: Veronica was waging civil war between her libido and her Bible. I was caught somewhere in the middle.

We first met at the only fitness center in town—a gym where I both worked and spent my free time. The place was a wreck, an establishment solely existing because the people of Belgrade, Montana, had nowhere else to exercise. A true monopoly on health. And this power of exclusivity led to poor management and customer disregard:

equipment suffered as foam burst from padded seams; volleyball courts vanished amongst invasive weeds; resigning employees were more common than new members. But I remained.

Veronica, a senior in high school, joined the gym during the latter half of my freshman year of college. I signed her up while establishing a flirtatious means of rapport, giving her an exclusive tour of the place and waving the initiation fee. She didn't seem to mind the awkward attention.

She had a shy air of virtue and innocent beauty. Veronica intrigued if only because I didn't recognize her— a rare thing in a town that small, especially a student of similar age. I can still envision the way she loitered with each entry, coy in keeping me company from across the counter—her half-smile revealing a seemingly permanent piece of chewing gum; her long golden hair cascading one shoulder to avoid covering the sign-in sheet; healthy and immaculate skin, cute glasses, oversized T-shirts still somehow doing her humble curves justice. She glowed— *overflowed*—with youth, vigor, and sexuality. Despite her bashful nature, she would guilelessly stare at me while lifting weights—mirrors confessing her yearnings. The passion became palpable. I was rearing, too. So I'd systematically, yet casually, address her in passing, always saying her name with intent: *Veronica—*

My God, I've forgotten how it feels to want something that bad, to lust for that mystery of life that can only linger—sweltering and lewd—between another's legs. The good days were when she came in.

I don't remember our first date, nor when we officially became a couple, but I remember being proud to call her mine. So I'd bring her around my high school wrestling buddies—making a spectacle of her exquisiteness—only to be teased about *finally* having a girlfriend. The jeering felt gratifying, though, a form of congratulations. Shane and Trevor, a pair of brothers who were like brothers to me, gaped at her beauty, damn near drooling while making Paleolithic grunts in response to her company. My family revered Veronica just the same, despite my pop's foul mouth causing her to cringe. Veronica's family was a different story.

They were cordial, her parents and three brothers, but from what Veronica told me in private, they didn't approve of me. Their passive rejection had nothing to do with me, per se; my faith (or lack of it) posed the critical issue. Veronica belonged to a family of conservative Christians living on the outskirts of town, and she attended a private school with a graduating class of maybe ten students, the reason I didn't recognize her at first. My family, on the other hand, didn't consider religion important enough to consider.

Despite this, I came to contemplate religion, well, religiously. Even got a university degree in it. But, as a child, growing up a non-Christian in a Christian country had me confused; without a base belief in the Bible (or any other sacred text) existential questions couldn't be easily answered or written off. No firm duality existed, only gray area. I wrestled with philosophy while other school kids, as awful as they can be, scorned me for my invisible ideological difference. This continual condemning led to a bitterness that spawned atheistic idealism, but not out of a self-understanding as much as an outward anger. If I was going to be branded a pagan, I was going to own the title.

My relationship with Veronica, forged by the temptation of adolescent attraction, was therefore the perfect setup for a disastrous high school heartache: a gamble of whether the pious or the pagan would come to the realization first.

With the passing of months, as with all blossoming love, luster gave way to reality—in our case, rival interpretations of a shared reality. Veronica began fretting over my eternal salvation. Began making an honest attempt to convert and save my soul—an effort consisting of educational videos explicating the science and rationality of Christianity. The film series was produced and narrated by a former atheist, a man who'd recently had a change of heart and now realized the errors of his ways. This narrator was to be a welcoming bridge for my transition as he explained the divine involvement of the earth's precise axial tilt, the perpetual pregnancy of kangaroos, and something to do with turtles. Veronica beamed while watching. (This type of behavior, I've come to learn, is aptly referred to as "missionary dating.")

My favorite conversion attempt came in the form of a book called *Answers to Tough Questions Skeptics Ask about the Christian Faith*. Of the nearly sixty questions addressed, some of the more compelling were: *Where do dinosaurs and other extinct animals fit into the biblical story?* and *Were the biblical miracles magic tricks which fooled the simple, primitive people?* I read with care, took notes, and found only greater resolve in my disbelief.

On the contrary, and despite Veronica's conservative upbringing and contempt for the profane, she loved secular cinema, especially things that seemed counterintuitive to her faith, such as *The Matrix*, *Stargate*, and *The Shield*. It was during an episode of *The Shield*, a violent police drama, that I had my most confusing interaction with her.

"I can't believe you watch this shi—stuff," I said, curling up to her in a blanket on her older brother's couch. "It's *so* gruesome!"

"It's so good though! You're gonna love this episode!" She'd already seen the season. What proceeded was this: someone being abducted, dismembered, and kept alive in a meat locker via tourniquets and medication.

"Oh my God," I whispered, my eyes widening. I sat with the perversion, wondering why my girlfriend enjoyed such violence—and, more so, wondering why the hell she thought *I* was going to enjoy it—but indulged in her interest nonetheless. Then, after saying goodbye and leaving the house, Veronica avoided me for a week. An explanation came when she dropped off a note at the gym. It revealed that in the height of my disgust I had used the Lord's name in vain: "*Oh my God.*"

This, as it turned out, upset Veronica more than the mutilation on the screen. Because the only thing more horrifying was an unrepentant sinner, a godless heathen— *me*—unknowingly rending her Jesus-loving heart to pieces. We moved past the transgression, thanks to a series of drawn-out late-night conversations, but not without the cost of debasing our hope in each other. I think we both knew the relationship wasn't going to work after that. What further compounded the religious war was sex.

I don't remember the first time we kissed, but I do remember it happened *a lot*. Her sexuality was repressed— a caged craving beating itself against the bars, shameless and aggressive, a carnal drive battling the conscience— and I became the erotic outlet. Her body a prison, my tongue the key. When the conscience won, as it always did, something strange happened: Veronica would cry.

She'd cry as we let our innocent hands wander, pacing our actions to her moral pain—fueled by the guilt—until she'd break, fleeing from the feelings, and leave me hanging in the passion of an elongated embrace to recite her good God's scripture. The first time she touched my penis, sliding eager fingers down my pants—skimming her purity ring across my erection—came with no satisfaction as she jolted back, as though burned, and retreated to her Bible. And let me tell you, watching a guilt-ridden girl rifle through the New Testament as a form of birth control, looking for any explanation to an inevitable hormone shift, was painful and far from arousing.

I began reading the Bible too, but only in the hopes of finding passages I could misconstrue into making intimacy sound acceptable. I would read Veronica these at the height of her breakdowns. And it worked—she beamed, so proud to hear the Lord's literature on my lips. So she'd press hers to mine. We kept on.

We kept on: her praying every night that I'd convert so we could marry and finally have guiltless relations, me content in just having a girlfriend even though the entire plight was ill-fated.

Things climaxed when I invited Veronica to attend a furniture convention in Cody, Wyoming. My parents have been in furniture my entire life, so to travel three and a half hours to a convention in celebration of this fact was nothing new to me. But to Veronica it was. The memories that remain are vivid: Veronica getting yelled at by a traveling rep for building a piece of display furniture wrong. Veronica getting upset at me for not defending her on the matter. I remember walking along the promenade of Old Trail Town, rustic boardwalks leading us hand in hand through homesteading history. And I remember Veronica telling me that if I ate the fresh onions on my dinner salad she would *not* be kissing me that night. I respected the wish, after a hard struggle over the decision, only to be rewarded in bed by advancing further than we'd ever gone before. She didn't even cry.

The world stood still that night as we naïvely explored sexuality. Summer heat hung in the air and off our naked bodies. Friends back home swam to tame the mounting temperature; others packed their belongings in preparation for an impending first year of college. High school sports were to become a relic of our past, and the word "friend" to become redefined by distance. Change lingered on the horizon as we all ignored the fact that once this heat dissipated, our teen years would vanish just the same. But on that night none of it mattered. Clothes off. Still chaste. Time stopping where her body fused to mine.

The next morning Veronica and I opted to skip the convention and explore the town—at least that's what we told my parents. We were in bed, naked again, playing at being emotionally compatible. Then I got an annoying call from my mother.

"Come eat lunch with us."

"We'll pass. Thanks though."

"Tyler, please come eat with us. *Please*." There resonated a vulnerability to her voice I'd never heard before. That voice—those words—now a broken record in my head. When we arrived everyone sat waiting outside: my parents, my older brother, his future wife. They had pressing news.

"What's up?" I said, looking from person to person.

"You should sit down," my dad replied.

"Seriously, what's going on?"

"Yesterday afternoon"—isolated tears formed in his eyes, spilling over and down his cheeks—"Shane drowned. Shane's dead, Tyler." In an unexplainable reaction I tried to run, turning directly into my mother's arms. And she clutched me tight—close—as a continental drift occurred at my core, like an unexpected earthquake rearranging my cosmology. This was the same shift Veronica had been fighting to create within me through her missionary-dating tactics—a readjustment of beliefs—except I now drifted further away.

Shane had died bridge jumping, drowning in a river we'd visited many times before. In fact, he'd called me to go with him. And what if I'd been there? What if I'd been home to say yes?—didn't matter now. Never did. That's how heartache works. The death could've happened to anyone: no alcohol involved, no strong current to fight, no protruding rocks to dodge. He simply over-rotated on a front flip and hit his head on the surface of the calm tributary. Concussed, he swam to the surface, smiled to our friends on the bridge, then sank—

And what if I'd been there? What if I'd been home to say yes? His body wasn't found for nearly four hours.

My tectonic shift resulted in the collapse of my assumed invincibility of youth: hurt became more than that of a high school hazing; loss more than that of a pet with feline leukemia. Because we are all led to believe—to worship the fact—that we can overcome the odds, become famous athletes, achieve considerable wealth, make failing relationships work. We're told *anything* is possible. But on those days when you see a father cry for the first time, having to tell his second son what death really means, you come to contemplate the fragility of not only life but worldviews.

My trust in hard truths fell apart, too. I realized that there is nothing invincible about us. That we're all going to put someone in the ground. Or they, you. That the core subatomic particle of this planet is the word goodbye—

and that goodbyes don't come easy. Because Shane was *supposed* to be alive. With me. With his brother and sister. His mother. His stepdad. And his death tore that family apart.

Veronica was wonderful through the whole process, driving me home from the convention early to be with mourning friends. She held and caressed me during the breakdowns; cooked me my favorite meals; undoubtedly prayed for everyone involved in the tragedy. But during those moments, when *I* was the one now crying in front of *her*, I accepted that we could never be together. I had no Bible to turn to, no scripture to guide me. Loss had become quantitative, and there was no greater plan at work. I didn't want to hear about a "better place" or about God calling Shane home. I couldn't allow that false comfort. And to me, my tears didn't contain any redemptive code to eternity or salvation, not the way Saint Veronica's did. Mine were droplets of water, sodium, and potassium. My sobs a requiem. A hymn for learning how to deal with heartache, over a water-wrinkled, decomposing—dead, dead, dead—drowned kid of eighteen.

I occasionally revisit the bridges of Gallatin County—the place where Shane died—and each summer I see new generations conducting the same rite of passage, launching their bodies from catwalk to water, as if coins into a fountain. Like things we forget to wish upon. Like fleeting youth taken for granted.

I don't remember how or when Veronica and I broke up, but I do know that the last time I saw her cry was the most difficult of our trials. It was the day we grew up and said goodbye.

✢

Lightning Over Las Cruces
(And for Those of Us That Knew Him)
Las Cruces, New Mexico

Jacob Watson, a local to the Las Cruces area, claims that storms like these only happen once a year: fabled Southwestern monsoons of New Mexico. And I believe it—all the folklore—considering the magnitude of this storm: lightning as the Second Coming; thunder, the end of days.

We watch in awe, Jacob at his home and the rest of us returning from a multi-day road trip—San Diego to God's country and back again. I'm convinced Texas got it wrong: God resides in New Mexico, the Old Testament fury before us as proof. The electric wrath is sporadic but constant, crashing against the panoramic horizon and illuminating a silhouette of the jagged Organ Mountains. At other times, bolts ricochet from one cloud to the next, cracking the sky horizontally and weaving a web set to catch all of our child-like wonder within. We became oblivious to anything separate from the storm—ourselves and each other. Mosquitoes preyed confidently on our flesh.

This is the lightning over Las Cruces. And the deadly percussion plays for hours.

A wedding brought us there. I'd been planning the road trip for months—and with the way I plan, there were detours aplenty: Saguaro National Park, White Sands National Monument, Carlsbad Caverns National Park, Guadalupe Mountains National Park. This desire to explore was a result of my time in Colorado and evolved into the goal of visiting every U.S. national park. Because something was still missing after failing to conquer Longs Peak and I needed to go further afield to find it, to move from the micro to the macro. I'd already crisscrossed the country several times—on wrestling trips, with Invisible Children, for graduate school—but now I wanted to be driven further, off the gridlocked web of interstate traverse, to the remote pockets of Americana set aside and preserved under the belief that wild ecology, as a link to forgotten sustainability, can be a respiratory solution to our choking progress. An answer to industrialism. And Guadalupe Mountains was helping me believe this, my thirty-third national park visited of the fifty-nine.

Once at the wedding though, we were only there to celebrate our friends and their commitment to each other: a ceremony, a future anniversary, a date to remember.

But I rarely fixate on dates: don't remember birthdays, don't remember holidays, for the most part I struggle to remember anything (a reason for multiple active journals). But I remember death days. I remember these as the culminations of every birthday and anniversary and special event ever celebrated. Because you only get one. I remember July 11. It was due in two days.

Every July I try to raise the dead. There are no incantations, no witches' brew, no charms or enchantments. My sorcery consists of revisiting photos and videos of a man who passed before his time. Occasionally there are tears, but more common are phone calls to others who knew him—Nate Henn, my target of resurrection.

But despite my efforts, I can't combat time, and memories are beginning to fade. Even more disconcerting, I question if the remaining memories are even accurate. This is why I summon the dead—necromancy each year on my solstice of sorrow—to enliven these fleeting recollections. And, when my witchcraft works, on days like today, Nate's ghost follows me across this country, begging for one more road trip, one last adventure. I understand why: travel slows us down, rekindles our senses, makes us focus on each other. His memory, our memories, they haunt me—but only when I let them.

I've been avoiding you, Nate, and because of this, the sad truth is, I've been forgetting you. Don't remember your laugh; don't remember the intricate details of your character; don't remember your favorite songs. There are no more idiosyncrasies. No more inside jokes. But I do know that I love you, or loved you. And now, when reluctantly trying to remember, all I return to is a video, produced by Invisible Children, that offers me a reduced version of you. But you are more than a movie, I'm convinced. My memories run deeper than that—but I can't remember why.

You're dead. It haunts me. And visiting the national parks isn't putting it to rest. Because six months before the explosion you told me about a girl who was on your radar. And as I got to know your coveted interest, I began flirting with her, innocent and playful, at least at first. But with every text and drawn-out gaze, a silent alarm was going off in my head. It wasn't the pursuit I despised—with pain in your eyes, Nate, you had encouraged me to date her—but it was my conscious act of betrayal.

By the time I kissed the girl, in a reckless drunken stupor, getting handsy behind a shady van in a San Diego parking lot, I knew the damage was done. And I hated what I'd done. What I was doing. It came from a rotten place—bad brain, bad heart, bad soul, I don't know. I yearned to offer you an apology, and I'd resolved to give you one after your return from Uganda—

I'm still avoiding you, trying to outrun your apparition. My shame. But on July 11, your death day, you always catch back up. In two days I'll be waiting for your storm to roll in. And I will remember. I'll remember all of those demons I've been suppressing. Remember that you are more than a tragic death. That July 11 does not define you. That I still owe you an abiding apology left unsaid.

There is lightning over Las Cruces as I look to my current traveling companions. I appreciate the honesty we've shared and the tales we've told; I watch fleeting energy illuminate their faces and I am glad we are here—no need for remembrance in the present.

I return to the storm. Begin scratching my bites. And I am certain Jacob is right: storms like these only happen once a year, and, sadly, for those of us who knew him, lightning never strikes the same place twice.

+

SELF-HARM SURVIVAL TECHNIQUES

"Survival is your own responsibility."

—The National Park Service

+

Brother of Eagle
Belgrade, Montana

————————

The severed head fell to our feet, first escaping its plastic grocery bag of containment, then tumbling down a dome of unkempt clothing—a burgeoning deposit of thrift-store loot—stockpiled in the back of a threadbare and dusty Ford Focus. A simple question followed: "You guys wanna see something cool?"

I nodded to our inquisitor, my uncle Donnie, knowing him dependable for the bizarre. Steve followed suit, trusting my judgment. Steve had arrived unfamiliar to Belgrade, Montana, having flown north to help me drive south. With San Diego as our destination and my future home, Steve and I had 1,200 miles to fill with national parks, outdoor festivals, and dive bars—roommates to be. Steve had never met my uncle but knew the stories. Now he bore witness to more than mythology. This was rural, this was ex-meth addicts, this was the mountains.

We stepped outside my parents' office building and ambled toward my uncle's decade-old beater. Opening the hatchback, Steve and I discovered the head: blackened beak, opulent eyes, feathers of a roasted hue. This red-tailed hawk arrived freshly dead and in pieces, one of which now laid at our feet. "Saw'm get hit on the Frontage Road on my way over," Donnie said, picking up the head—bare hands—and reuniting it with the bulk of the carcass. "Still warm when I got to it."

This fulfilled the bizarre I expected, though sullen. Looking to Steve, I worried about his reaction, but his expression spoke of appreciation. I felt pride. "Wanna take a feather?" Donnie offered.

They were sturdy and difficult to pluck, hollow quills once gifting this lifeless predator the miracle of flight and a dangerous grace to sanctify it—a juxtaposition of resilience and fragility, menace and elegance. Dull colors of red, white, and black insinuated maturity; horizontal bands displayed perfect form like ripples on a pond. I pinched the feather at the base and spun it like a fallen leaf. "What are you gonna do with the body?" I asked.

"The Shaman," was all Donnie said.

Montana is long winters rewarded with perfect summers, the seasons never clearly marked by a calendar, only instinct. Blood from the nose meant hay from the fields: fall. Wildflowers in the valley meant water from the snowpack: spring. And these harsh seasons maintained a soothing rhythm for the farmland—even the brutal winters played their role in sustaining the ecosystem. With such patterns it's inevitable you'll notice how things die and mulch and decay. How they regrow.

It was commonplace, my upbringing, but Belgrade remains the nerve center to my atlas; if I was to prick a finger in Montenegro my mountains would feel it in Montana. What a place to come from: danger was climbing a ponderosa pine; fear, spraining an ankle in a gopher hole. Friends resided within a bike-ride radius while school teachers doubled as your local grocer. My neighbors were enchanting characters, too: Mr. Hoffman, a man just shy of one-hundred, had the vigor and tenacity of someone half that age; and Sarah, a young adventurer, kept an angelic smile despite the haunting scars of a grizzly attack. Both beautiful in their natural afflictions.

In later years, however, the neighborhood succumbed to low-income housing and a dodgier draft of neighbor. Trailers overtook lots, like weeds, where houses once stood. Strange violence and dirty drugs became a more realistic danger than the bucolic outdoors. One codger mowed the lawn in a Speedo, his bony body repulsive against the summer sun. Another was assaulted with a baseball bat in his sleep—the assailant never discovered, but his ex-wife is still the prime suspect. Enchantment waned.

Because of this, when my father, Bruce, encountered a bizarre little man lingering in the alley behind our house, he approached warily. The stranger wore Native American garb: moccasins, denim jeans, a beaded jacket with the traditional pixilated patterns of larkspur petal blue and sumac berry red. Long gray hair grazed his shoulders, thick glasses brought age to an already aging face, and a bowler hat (also with Native beads) completed the visage. The man introduced himself as Terry "Brother of Eagle Shaman." He wanted to know about our hawks.

In my parents' backyard resided two blue spruce trees, both towering at least fifty feet in their maturity. In the southern tree a pair of red-tailed hawks regularly returned and nested each summer, a presence reminded by their war shrieks piercing the mountain silence. Entrails of prey littered the lawn (we worried for our Chihuahuas). Terry revered the birds, explaining their nesting and mating habits with encyclopedia-like detail. He could tell, even from the distance of the alley, that one hawk was missing a sole tail feather. He asked my father to bring him the absent plume if ever found—*could be used for a ceremony*, he said.

The two ended up talking for hours, with my father learning, to great surprise, that Terry had lived in the neighborhood for years. Terry had kept busy working for a power company, but due to the recession was forced into an early retirement and now spent his time at home, walking around the neighborhood to quell the feral boredom. Hawks kept his attention.

But watching raptors was nothing new to Terry; in fact, it's how he'd earned his name. Here's the fable: during his shaman training, Terry sought mentorship from a powerful medicine man—a man who'd confessed Terry's spirit too weak for the tasks required of the religious position. Distraught, Terry drove home in a haze, encouraged only by the sight of a bald eagle circling his house. The next morning Terry watched a news report regretting the death of a bald eagle on the Frontage Road. Terry returned to the medicine man to ask the meaning of the omen, to which he was informed that the eagle had sacrificed its life to strengthen Terry's spirit—to make him a shaman. From that point on Terry was known as "Brother of Eagle Shaman."

My dad eventually found the missing tail feather and,

as promised, brought it to Terry. Our surprised neighbor, out of gratitude, then offered to evaluate my father's spirit by performing a special ritual. My dad of course declined, being a no-nonsense type of man, but a friendship formed nonetheless.

My dad often scoffed at the Shaman's antics, confused by his antiquated worldview, but, as with most of the things Bruce belittles, he had an unspoken soft spot for the strange guy. He would simultaneously complain about the Shaman's long rants as he started walking across the street to chat with him. When these interactions did occur, every couple of months, the Shaman would, without fail, invite my family to a ritual at his house with the promise of bison meat and hawk talk. These meetings took place in a tipi that towered above Terry's humble blue mobile home. A smaller structure soon joined the yard as well: a sweat lodge. That was the first summer.

The following summer the hawks had chicks, but died after emerging from their eggs. Terry became visibly bothered, lamenting the loss and wishing he could've given them a proper send off. The chicks died again the subsequent summer, but this time Bruce climbed to the top of the grand spruce tree (with my mom squawking about the danger while concurrently taking pictures) to claim the deceased from the nest. He brought one body down, contorted like a dried-out novelty shop horror, as well as the failed eggs, and gave them to Brother of Eagle Shaman. Smoke billowed from his tipi that afternoon. A burial that evening.

Images of our nesting hawks appeared in an autobiography Terry self-published that same year, titled *The Calling of a Shaman and His Visions*. He delivered a signed copy to Bruce one day while at work. Terry knew the quality of the book to be poor, the copy editing terrible, but he left the book the way it was—*a true representation of my story*, he said.

Skimming through the pages, you'll find Terry's recollections of growing up in Maryland, joining the Air Force, and serving in the Vietnam War. You'll find disclosures about his discomforts with living in the "white man's world," about losing the love of his life to unknown reasons, and about finding long-sought refuge in the mountains of Montana. The book takes on a more mystical mood when Terry discusses having "a bleed on the brain at age fifty." He claims it killed him. He also claims to have surprised doctors by bringing himself back to life—so our fable goes.

The latter half of the book is about Terry getting the calling to become a shaman—a calling, he says, that would have ended his life if left ignored. He, of course, answered the call and started "a long chain of events" that led to the writing of his book. He was proud of his work. And my family, strangely, felt proud too. So when Unc Donnie brought the decapitated hawk to the Shaman, it really came as no surprise—that's where birds went for burial.

The morning after Donnie showed us the dead raptor, Steve slept while I packed my Hyundai Santa Fe for the journey ahead, for a new and renewed life in San Diego. I'd settled in that town once before but wanted to give it another try. My call to migration.

The air cut crisp and brittle that morning—not cold but reminiscent of winter's approach. My dad helped prepare my car, not saying much, only looking despondent. In the process of struggling to load a heavy stationary bike into the backseat, a strange man moseyed across the street to join us. My dad whispered, *It's him . . . the Shaman.*

That was my first time meeting Terry; all prior knowledge had come through stories. He proved different than I'd imagined. His attire and countenance were the same as in the photographs I'd seen, but he stood shorter. Rounder. He seemed older in some ways. Younger in others. When it came to rhetoric, however, Terry achieved the hype. He talked without prompt. Sometimes without audience.

My father and I wrestled with the bike, contorting and adjusting it to the will of the car, getting nowhere. All the while, the Shaman waxed feverishly about rain dances and healing ointment. He circled the car, gesturing the words with his hands and the expressions with his face. It was almost a performance, and he'd earned his crowd—we submitted our attention.

He spoke of a pow-wow the previous weekend, of leading dozens of healing ceremonies and participating in Native music. He laughed and smiled, recalling the rhythm with his clapping hands, living in his own whimsical world. When the beat eventually stopped, he became serious with the stilling of his movement. He spoke of a bison skull, his speech slow and methodical.

"This skull had incredible spirit," he said, "and I knew I had to find the right person to oversee it. That's why, during a grand ceremony, I presented it to a fifteen-year-old boy. He was troubled, lost in his way, but I knew the bison would guide him. He promised whole-heartedly to protect the skull. That ceremony brought me to ninety-five percent. I'm a ninety-five-percent shaman now."

My father chimed in, sarcastic, "What are you gonna do to get that last five percent?"

"Oh, it's hard to say," Terry responded in sincerity.

"When I started I was about forty-five percent. I've done hundreds of ceremonies to get where I am. This hawk burial tonight may help. Will your family be attending? Would love to have the company."

"We're a little busy today, but let us know how it goes. We gotta get this guy packed and on the road." My dad squeezed my shoulder, eyes welling.

"Safe travels," Terry said. "I'll say a Cherokee prayer for you."

Later that morning Steve, Donnie, and I rode vintage bikes around town, all from my uncle's collection. It was Fall Festival, a rural celebration of the change of season, and the town came to life with artisan vendors and food carts. That afternoon I left Belgrade to a tearful good-bye. I'd left my family many times before, but this exodus somehow felt different—I think we all knew it wasn't a temporary departure. While the city parade began congesting the streets, I vanished once again from the town that had reared me.

I took Steve to Yellowstone, showing him the relics of my youth, showing him what it means to have the mountains both in your blood and in your backyard. I showed him wonderment and awe, geysers and grizzlies. The forgotten hours of that first night found us resting in Provo, Utah.

The next morning, while trudging through the road construction of a fleeting southern Utah summer, my dad called. "You're not gonna believe this, but the Shaman's dead. He killed himself last night."

"Are you . . . what happened?"

"I don't know. He came over and talked to your mom last night, just hours before he did it, saying how much pain he'd been in, with his aneurisms and all. It's almost like he was just waiting to become a full shaman." This time there was no sarcasm in my dad's voice.

As further details surfaced, the suicide made more sense. According to friends and neighbors, Terry had contemplated self-destruction regularly, living in perpetual pain from chronic headaches. Every day was a battle for him, they said. And he'd fought with vigor. The books he wrote, the stories he shared, the ceremonies he performed—these were his legacy, his gifts to the greater good. His exit, as well, had become a ceremony in itself: he wore his finest Native American outfit, wrapped up tight in a traditional blanket. And despite wherever his soul went after rising through the top of that tipi, his discarded shell stayed behind with the rest of us.

Terry had buried a hawk—found by my uncle—that previous day. He'd given it a proper send off. It's hard to say if he did the same for himself, but both creatures returned to nature equally, both strengthening the spirits of those in need. Terry must have reached one-hundred percent that day. He must have thought his work here was done, or at least, that he had done enough. And there is no doubt, based on his astuteness, that he recognized the three tail feathers missing from that last hawk he was to ever put in the ground. He may have simply thought this another result of the collision—after all, the bird came in pieces. Or, with all his eccentric wisdom, he may have known they were plucked and stolen from their rightful owner. Either way, I can't help but look at this hollow feather and wonder about the weight it holds: a curse, a blessing, just the remnants of a dying worldview. I pinch the feather at the base with my fingers. I spin it. I spin it like a fallen leaf.

✦

Snowmen Matter (Hard Winters)
Bozeman, Montana

─────────

Abel says, "You'd be the worst person in the world to prevent a suicide. I hope no one ever asks you for help." It's not an insult, though. It's kind of funny. But, well, I'm not laughing—I'm thinking about John, having killed himself a week or so earlier. I get why he did it. I get it. But Abel doesn't get *me*: I was only confessing that I understood where John was coming from, defending the merits of mixing a lethal dose of chemicals into a toxic plume of death inside his black Jeep Liberty. I was defending him. Not a crime, right?

Abel's not appeased. But this, I can tell you, is because he knows nothing of the matter, none beyond what his religious institution has told him:

Suicide is selfish.

Suicide is blasphemy.
Suicides go to hell.

I'm not surprised, I guess—Abel's the type of guy who criticizes the way people floss. The type who cringes to curse words and doesn't trust people who smoke pot. The type of guy who smugly corrects your grammar in public. That type.

So we're in the kitchen, discussing John, and he's like, "Killing yourself is bad, killing yourself is bad." And he's saying this like a true asshole because *he* doesn't know *he's* using improper grammar—yourself is a reflexive pronoun and I want to shout, WHERE'S THE FUCKING AN-TECEDENT! But I don't correct people in public, not like him, so I keep my mouth shut, right, because it's polite and not the time for being petty.

I keep it all in my head.

Shit.

I don't know what I'm saying. I forgot about that whole invisible "you" thing. The imperative form. So Abel's right. Again.

And to think I want to be a writer.

I'm a piece of shit.

I'm a piece of shit. And he's right.

I should kill myself.

No.

Maybe.

Yes, he's right, but only this once, only grammatically, because wanting to die is like a gift from God—or what-ever—that some of us are given. Not everyone gets to experience the tragic miracle of this grisly craving and, therefore, not everyone can understand it; it's just something you get or you don't. But convincing someone with a healthy brain to believe otherwise would be like trying to explain homosexual tendencies to a staunch, anti-gay redneck. It's a cancer joke to a survivor. An Auschwitz joke to a Jew. A burger to a bulimic. Some things just aren't funny to some people. And suicide is a tough joke to get.

What Abel doesn't know is that I used to play this game called "I'm Gonna Kill Myself Today." You know the game: the one where you collect all the knives in the house and line them up on the kitchen table in front of you, dozens of them, all shimmering and crisp—well, when your roommates do their FUCKING DISHES.

Anyway, that's how the game starts—blades on the table—and then you pick 'em up, one by one, baby, and feel the weight, examine the sharp ends. Most are too dull to do any damage but there is an added drama to having abundance—it's the American way! Some blades are perfect though, and they mix in well with the rest—junk knife, serious knife, junk knife, serious knife. Some are sentimental: a hunting knife I grab when I get spooked at night; or my pocket knife, an Old Timer, which my pops got me for Christmas; or the entire kitchen set my mom got me when I moved away.

Next, you imagine what it's like to run the serious ones across your skin, the underside of your forearms, or maybe even to let them penetrate you, a quick thrust right around where you believe the heart to be: cut, cut, slice, slice, stab, stab. It's fun and, with the right attention span, you can play for hours.

But who has the "right" attention span? Right? Especially when you're thinking about ending it all—that's actually when it's the hardest to concentrate on *anything* worth concentrating on. You forget about the good stuff: hikes through Yellowstone with your little brother, teaching him how to identify water hemlock; teaching him how to survive a grizzly attack. Playing football with your nephews, running across your parents' lawn in a feigned effort to tackle them—you wanna see 'em score. Or how good those days feel when it doesn't hurt to breathe, to think, to look toward the future with optimism. You forget.

What's worse is when you start worrying that your roommates are going to come home and find you with *all the knives*—and, oh God, I forgot, Bert has this amazing knife, some sort of samurai ninja shit that could cut through *anything*. Pennies and soda cans and frozen meat—like those demonstrations on TV. Because being a chef, Bert needs the good stuff. And we, as his lowly roommates, *are not allowed to touch that knife!*

So I'm like, a little panicked, right, sitting in front of these knives—Bert's knife—thinking about how comforting they are and how good they would feel, but if Bert were to walk in and find me with his knife—*holy shit!*—he would he be pissed. Just imagine the look on his face if I soiled that thing! So I get spooked, right, and I start thinking about putting my macabre collection away—but God, I feel safe having the knives right in front of me. Because to put them away means I have to keep living. And I don't think I want that. I pick one up—

Here's my secret: there is nothing good in my heart. Such a rotten piece of flesh. I wrote a poem about it:

> I can't stop ordering books from Amazon.
> Can't stop checking Facebook.
> Can't stop snacking on junk food.
> Can't stop letting the big things slide.
> And the small things destroy me.
> I can't stop thinking about suicide.

Can't stop watching porn.

Can't stop being nice to people.

      When I don't want to be.

I can't stop from reading slow.

Can't stop from checking the mail.

      Each time I pass the mailbox.

I can't stop believing things could have been better.

Can't stop from feeling like a failure.

Can't stop scouring online dating sites.

Can't stop writing.

Can't stop hoping that my stories matter.

      That I matter.

I can't stop listening to Placebo.

Can't stop thinking about suicide.

Can't stop watching porn.

Can't stop repeating myself.

      Day.

      After day.

      After day—

Shit! My roommates! Goddamn them and their ability to come home at all the wrong times. So, one by one by one, ever slowly, reluctantly, the blades start going back to their rightful places: sheaths, cupboards, wooden blocks—

I take them back out—

I need this!—

No—

I don't wanna die—

Fuck. I do—

I don't—

I *want* this—

I hate myself—

I don't—

I do—

I'm scared—

But GODDAMNIT! Bert's knife feels *so* good—

Bert! He could get home any minute! I put them away: sheaths, cupboards, wooden blocks. And that's when I get really scared. Terrified. I'm shaking. I'm alone. Worst of all, I'm alive.

The last time this happened—the whole "I'm Gonna Kill Myself Today"—was after an Invisible Children Christmas party where the girl I liked wasn't giving me the attention I wanted. Instead, she was drunk in the corner and grinding on some dude, my occasional glance catching the back of her swooping dress revealing the contours of her slender shoulders. Really grinding into that crotch.

So I got the knives out that night. And put them away. Got them out. Put them away—

I'll never be good enough, I'm convinced. I first realized this in high school, when I really learned how to hate myself. So I've earned the right to die, right? Thirteen years of this agony?

No. Not yet.

Instead, I made a call:

"Mom, I need help."

"I know, Tyler. I'm here." She gets this a lot. I scare her, that type of scare only a parent with an unstable child would understand. She didn't know what else to say, or the magnitude of the situation, but her silence was enough. She listened to me breathe for a while, ear to receiver, the sound of a human life still surviving. Somehow.

I stopped drinking for a long while after that, alcohol being my supreme advocate to play "the game." I've stopped with the knives altogether. But Abel doesn't know any of this, and he doesn't know that for us suicidals it's a fucking war, and if you've never been through *this* war, well then you can SHUT YOUR DAMN MOUTH—because you haven't earned the right to tell me life is worth living if you've never had the courage to think it might actually be worth dying.

The nerve of some people, right?

Years later I finally get my grand opportunity to spit in Abel's face. A friend wants to die and I'm like, "Thank fucking God!"

It starts while I'm watching a movie. First, a text: *I'm gonna kill myself.* You know, typical cry-for-help bullshit. I keep watching.

Then: *I need help.* Yada, yada, yada.

Okay fine, I think, I'll call him when I get to a good stopping point. But he beats me to it. I pick up.

"Tyler," the voice on the other side of the line stammers, "I need you to tell my family I love them—tell my parents, my sister and brother. Tell them it isn't—"

"What are you talking about?" I'm half engaged.

"I'm doing it tonight." He's drunk.

"Where are you?"

"The cemetery."

"You have a weapon?"

"A knife." Hah, my kinda dude!

"All right, I'll be there in fifteen. Don't do anything stupid, all right? Don't do anything till I get there."

"Okay."

"Promise me."

"Okay."

"Promise me."

"Okay, geez, I promise!"

I arrive at Lindley Park, the entrance to the burial

grounds. It's dark. A real eerie vibe. I kill my engine just outside the cemetery and peer into the shadows: stone fence, iron gate, abject darkness. Joseph is in there, I know it, and he's on like, five meds. There's a knife in there too—

Fuck. What if this becomes one of those murder/suicide things? The dude is pretty unstable.

"Joe?" I croak, not getting any closer to the gate.

Silence.

"Joe?"

Silence.

And then a figure. A walkin' dude. A black silhouette against all the snow, some lightly falling and blanketing the hallowed grounds, and he is ambling like a creature from the damn island of Dr. Moreau. Definitely drunk.

"Joe?"

"Yeah?" His speech is slurred.

"You okay?"

"No." He's close.

"Where's that knife, buddy?"

"Here." He pats his zipped-up winter jacket. He's upon me.

"Can I have it?" He says nothing, just unzips. And my brain is screaming, *You're about to get stabbed, you shithead!* But he hands me the blade—it's in my hands, just like the old days. This thing is *way* bigger than Bert's knife, holy hell—

But then he assaults me. And he's strong, that kind of freak strength you don't want to mess with, and I'm overtaken. I thrash. I flail. But it's useless. I succumb.

It takes me a minute to realize I'm being hugged. Being loved. That he's crying. Weeping. Blubbering something. That I'm crying too. Not weeping. Blubbering nothing.

This goes on a while until I ask him if I can put the

knife away, empathetic and knowing how hard it is to sometimes let these things go. He agrees. I bury it under the rock climbing crash pad in the back of my Sante Fe.

"Okay, asshole," I say, "put on your gloves."

"Why?"

"What does it look like? We're building a snowman."

"Why?" Despite the confusion he's on his knees, ready to participate. No gloves.

"Just help." He does, and the small orbs become bigger, leaving a path behind like rolled carpet, all that gross shit underneath: dead grass, mud, mulch.

"What do you want, Joe?"

"Huh?"

"In life. What do you want in life?"

"Doesn't matter." He's fumbling but rolling snow.

"It might not, but what comes to your mind first?"

"I can't get into grad school."

"Does that define you—your self-worth? I mean, if you could do *anything*—if you could wake up tomorrow with no obligation, would you still be trying to get into school or something else? What would you do?"

"Paint."

"Paint?"

"Yeah, paint." A torso ball gets lifted to the larger foundation ball.

"Paint what?"

"Anything."

"Then why don't you fuckin' paint?" A head ball gets lifted to the torso ball.

"It's not that easy, Tyler. I can't just wake up tomorrow and do what I want—there's too much pressure. I'm nothing." This last part he whispers to himself. I'm nothing too. But I don't tell him.

"Why are you so down on yourself again?" But I know why. I get the joke.

"Parents. Society. Girlfriends. What happened to me when I was younger . . ." We're collecting and analyzing branches. Picking up stones.

"Do you know why I dropped out of graduate school?" I say.

"No."

"The Mayan prophecy."

"That end-of-days shit?" he asks.

"Yeah. You remember. I was a teaching assistant down in Florida helping with an Intro to Religion course. So, one day, we're teaching end-time theology—all of it, including the Mayan stuff—and on the walk back to the office my professor says, 'You know, if any of those kids actually believed in the prophecy they wouldn't be here. They wouldn't graduate before the world ended.'

"Then he looks at me, right, and says, 'If you knew for certain the world was going to end tomorrow would you still be doing what you're doing today?' And emphatically, without hesitation, I said no. And this festers. I can't stop thinking about it. Because I'm miserable—one of the most depressed times in my life—and I can't stop thinking: Why would I waste a single day? Why would I invest so much time now in academic misery with the simple hope and gamble on a happy future—because what if it never comes? I should be happy *now*.

"So I left. Dropped out. Haven't wasted a single day since. And it's the best decision I've ever made."

He looks like he's gonna puke. Definitely gonna puke. But no, he's planting twig arms into the snow body instead. "Not everyone can just drop everything," he responds. "If I don't get into school I don't know what I'm gonna do."

"Either you get in or you don't. None of it matters. It just doesn't. You know what matters?"

"What?"

"This"—I point to what we've created, only missing a carrot nose. "Do you remember how easy it was as a kid? You just built snowmen for the sake of building a snowman. No pressure, no expectation, no false idea that it was ever going to last. Because none of this lasts. So just enjoy it. Because if I was to die tomorrow I wouldn't regret what I did today: built a snowman with you.

"Paint if you want to, Joe. Become a dentist, a lawyer, whatever. Do what makes you *happy*. And don't worry, I'm not gonna feed you that bullshit of 'Everyone loves you' or 'You have so much to live for,' but if you do want to kill yourself, you have to make me a promise."

"Yeah?"

"Two things, actually."

"What?"

"You have to be sober: not an ounce of alcohol, or drugs, or anything in your blood."

"Okay."

"And you have to do the dirty work yourself. You have to tell your family and friends *yourself*. As soon as you can explain to them why you don't think life is worth living, then you can do it. And don't you dare ever ask me to do it for you again. *Ever*. That shit isn't fair. It's cowardly."

"Sorry."

"It's fine."

"Sorry."

"How you feeling?"

"Better."

"You ready to go? You're staying with me tonight."

"Okay. Yeah, I'm ready." We start walking toward the

car. "Hey, Tyler."

I turn to look at him—and get assaulted again. Another hug.

"Thank you."

"Don't worry about it." More tears.

"No, listen, if I didn't have you to call, someone who really understands what it's like, I'd be dead right now. You're the only person I could have called tonight. You're the only person that could've saved my life. Thank you."

Joe would go on to get into grad school. Would find a proper balance with his meds. Become healthy, successful, happy even. Still painting. Still building snowmen with me whenever he comes home to visit. But all I could think about in that "Thank You" moment, of all the things in the entire universe to think about, was that fuckwad Abel. I wanted to call him up and rub that shit IN HIS SMUG LITTLE FACE. But I didn't. Not a peep. Because, I guess, considering the circumstances, that would have seemed petty or trivial or something. Because, well, he'd already missed the punch line. And I'd never actually want Abel to understand the joke.

+

Blood Ties
Wisdom, Montana

———————

When my dad asked me not to kill myself, standing on top of Homer Young, he asked without asking. As a faithful son, I've asked him too, without asking, to never leave me. *I'm scared to live without you*, we keep saying to each other, without saying it, over and over, and over and over.

This is a love story. Like most love stories, this one is neither simple nor easy . . .

On June 19, 1977, Bruce stumbled into the Flying J truck stop sometime around midnight—his eighteenth birthday—and asked to use the phone. *Dad*, he said to the receiver, *I need you to come get me*. They hadn't spoken much, the father and son, not since Bruce left town. The lull wasn't due to inconsideration or a result of being too busy, but by design. Bruce was still busted up by his parents confessing their divorce at his high school graduation.

This declaration was the culmination of small-town betrayal and office-space infidelity. In all honesty though, there wasn't any surprise in this overwrought and overripe recipe to the tragic. Only bad timing. When Bruce should have been receiving gifts for the academic feat no one thought he'd achieve, he was given this: a broken home, now with the proper separation to prove it.

Not being a family of many words, Bruce left—to California—to let the physical manifestation of pain and hurt and anger and deception and dissidence transubstantiate into the tangible act of travel. I've learned a lot from the man. Because, if only in appearance, I was there. You see, Bruce was wearing my face, a genetic code I'd inherit seven years later. Our mark of replication. I was there—potential energy hidden in his cells—somehow already drawing on his lessons. The first: how to break your own heart.

When he came back to Montana, after weeks of coastal camping with a girlfriend, he found himself at that familiar Belgrade truck stop and ready to make a call. The overnight attendant refused the service, insisting, instead, they hail an ambulance. My dad, Bruce, blood soaked and trailing glass across the tile floor—from his hands, his face, any exposed skin—was the walking dead.

He'd rolled his 1953 Ford truck five times through a potato field after falling asleep at the wheel. Not surprising, as my dad had an ongoing history of misconduct, accruing plenty of early opportunities to end our family lineage—his own biological legacy—well before I was invited onto that genealogical hardwood tree. Bolts of lightning just missed him while bailing hay during a rural summer job. Revenge-thirsty assholes jumped him after being offended by his arrogant attitude and sharp tongue at a bowling tournament. Snarling coyotes circled him after accidentally wandering into their den while hunting in the Bridger Range. But that night, the night his truck rolled, was the closest my dad would get to snuffing out my existence long before I ever existed.

He came away from the accident with broken legs, broken arms, a snapped collar bone, crushed ribs, a punctured lung, a ticket for reckless driving, and a restored relationship with his parents. All this, of course, was counted as lucky, because, if you know anything about old Ford trucks, it's that they're built like tanks, with an industrial steel frame protecting the integrity of the automobile, but doing little to defend the bodies within. My dad was thrown from the truck, through the thick windshield, and clear of the carnage before the violent revolutions began. His chic jean jacket protected him from a full baptism in shards of shattered glass that mostly lodged in his face. Considering the severity of his injuries, it took him hours to walk from the wreck to the truck stop, though only a mile away, where he made that call. *Dad*, he said to the receiver, *I need help.*

The old Ford—some forty-years later—sits outside the emergency exit door of my bedroom. Me, living in a make-shift furniture store that my parents own and operate. The backyard, a thin strip of weed-laden grass growing between a corrugated tin wall and a chain-link fence, is where junk accumulates. You'll find things once-used but now seemingly useless: stacks of spare tires, tricycles meant for toddlers, raised-box garden beds I've had the seasonal intentions of using but never do. This all sets the backdrop for a truck that doesn't move.

It's canary yellow—though I believe it to have been white the night it rolled—with exhaust stacks rising alongside the cab doors and running boards adding style to the unemotional machine. I know little of cars, having no heart for things ascribed culturally masculine, but I do know that this one is badass. Strangers come by trying to buy it, to barter. You'd never suspect it'd once been demolished and rebuilt, rolled and raised from the dead.

I often wonder what Bruce sees when looking at the old relic, when turning away potential buyers, never confessing that his sentiment isn't for sale. I often wonder what rabbit hole of memories such an artifact can send him down—to the night of the wreck? To the road trip before? Further yet even?

My dad grew up in Bozeman, Montana—never really left—and became a farm kid: bailing hay, raising pigs, fighting as sport. He had a pet raccoon.

The animal, later named Penelope, only a cub when found orphaned near a favorite fishing hole, was taken home to be fostered. Any admirer of the wild would have done the same. That or fetch a gun.

The raccoon ate cereal with my dad and his siblings, all still children, sitting at the table, washing her hands before and after just the same. She'd rummage through cabinets when unaccompanied, open a window when needing to go outside, and slept in bed with my dad, often making purrs to the safety of having a home, to the comfort of companionship. But raccoons are volatile creatures, and once Penelope started experiencing the inevitable hormone changes of adulthood, she got mean, demanding

Lucky Charms at all hours of the day and biting Bruce when he'd stop her from perusing the Lazy Susan. She started avoiding most humans altogether, staying out all night yet still sleeping at the snug distance of the front-yard trees. She later left, without warning or goodbye, back to the wild in which she was found.

My dad changed too, segueing from an after-school fishing aficionado to a small-town sports idol. A football running back, and nasty as hell, he once played a whole high school season—the year they lost state—with a broken forearm.

This mean streak spilled over into his personal life too: he'd get into bar fights with anyone looking at him wrong. A time when you'd pummel someone simply for being gay, or ethnic, or a hippie. My father fell into the latter of the three—but only in appearance, not ideology—with long, wavy hair gracing his shoulders. The drinking age was lower then and the tolerance for violence higher. Bruce beat the shit out of a lot of people.

He womanized. Drank too much. Worked a blue-collar job and slowly moved his way up the chain of command at a local furniture store due to infectious charm and proven work ethic. It was impossible then, much as it still is today, not to desire his approval despite a quiet and reserved disposition.

All this, the drinking and fighting and bigotry, was no anomaly to Montana, and, therefore, when my dad accidentally impregnated my mother, a just-graduated cheerleader of the same high school, it wasn't a rarity either. The progression of events led to a courthouse wedding (not the most romantic of genesis stories, but the onset of a lasting love), and the arrival of my older brother. I joined the family two years later—my birth planned—and became the fourth member of a humdrum trailer-park home lost in a community called Hidden Valley. It wasn't until I started the second grade that we moved to our split-level house in Belgrade, just miles away from Bozeman but isolated in its separation, where I'd spend the rest of my childhood and adolescence.

I didn't fit the mold of a typical Montana kid, not when compared to that of the generations before me. The contention eroded my self-worth, and, because of this, by high school I started having troubles of my own, but nothing familiar to those of my father. I never had a thirst for booze or an issue with juggling women. I never knew the qualms of being too popular or the pressures of being athletic. My troubles stemmed from the absence of these things: from being reared a Dunning but somehow failing the unspoken expectation of carrying the name.

At fourteen, my brain shifted—collapsing in upon itself—adding me to that all-too-common statistic of just another kid with clinical depression. At that time, I understood little of what was happening to the physiology of my mind. I only knew that validation had somehow become an external thing, and I wasn't getting it from my peers or my community or any of the pretty girls with their fresh and newly formulated curves. Thoughts of self-harm would creep in as I sprawled across the bathroom floor for hours, the door locked out of shame, blankets wrapped tightly around my head, hoping to somehow subdue the sensation of rodents clawing from inside my skull. The feeling of drowning just beneath an unbreachable surface.

I started cutting my forearms because, although I couldn't understand the pain in my head, it became real when seeping from little slits in my skin. I was bleeding myself back to existence. And it felt relieving to have something to confirm. Because claiming depression can be like proving a ghost—no one wants to believe you.

There were times I'd skip school dances or sporting events for the comfort of being alone, only to face questioning:

"Why aren't you going?"

"Don't feel good."

"The flu?"

"No. Depressed."

"Depressed?" my mom would echo. "I thought maybe you were *actually* sick." My dad, less enthused: "What the fuck do you have to be sad about?"

Like my dad, I was slow to ask for help, especially after learning the staunch rules of the American West—you get through your shit *alone*. Even after you've broken damn near every bone in your body and have walked to the local truck stop, even after you've refused an ambulance ride due to a stubborn fear of dying in the accursed thing, you still find it hard to ask for help. I'm stubborn, too.

But stubbornness, for me, was never an ambulance ride. It was the psychotherapy I never got. Those antidepressants I never took. And this stubbornness led to my closest encounters with death. Because depression can be a car wreck, getting tossed and thrown upon every impact of a misfired—or maybe just missing—neurotransmitter. Glass gets stuck in your face. Bones get broken. You walk, for miles and miles and miles, each day, wounds festering, passing thoughts becoming a salt to the lesions, no aid on the horizon. You become the living dead.

Depression is confusing to watch, I understand this, the way one cyclically wages civil war against themselves. The way someone self-harms to stay alive. It's easy to accidently say hurtful things out of frustration:

I thought maybe you were actually sick.

What the fuck do you have to be sad about?

This doesn't mean that understanding is unachievable, from one generation to the next, from one father to a son. We've had different relationships with death, Bruce and I, but we've both made that same stubborn walk, both made that same prudent call: *Dad, I need help.*

I look to Bruce: a man who never took shit from anyone, labored endless hours to take his burgeoning family from a trailer park to a split-level house to a dream home on an acre of land. This is a man who could drink and get mean, drive throughout the night without succumbing to sleep, and gave me a piggyback ride to bed every night when I was still small enough to bear. This is a man I've seen become more patient and understanding, be more generous than anyone I know, and has taught me the importance of living a life worthy of explanation. He's never missed an event, sporting or otherwise, of any of his kids or grandkids. He's taken up birdwatching so he'd have a reason to pursue national parks with me. He still tells me factual tall tales on all road trips.

"You know, Penelope came back once," he recently said, "nearly a year after running away. She came back—with three cubs—and waited for me on the porch while I was at school. When I got home she showed me her kids, not letting me get too close, and then left. I never saw her again."

Or: "I really respect why you became a vegetarian. I think, now, if I was to start up hunting again I wouldn't bring a gun. I'd only shoot animals with my camera."

I see fissures forming in his tough exterior the older he gets. He'll cry when saying *I'm proud of you.* He'll slip money in my pockets when he knows I can't afford to eat. He still writes "Home" in the margins of Montana when giving me road maps (yes, he still uses road maps).

I see fissures, for the better, maybe—less racist, less violent, less obscene—but they allude to the inevitable: impermanence. Here's the conundrum: though wanting to die myself, I don't want *him* to die. More aptly, I'm scared to live without him. Because I've seen what losing a parent does to a child—through the examples of my partially orphaned friends—like when an aneurism steals life without warning, or when cancer makes its slow multi-year march across the fading humility of a dignified death, or when suicide leaves the reminder that sometimes life just isn't worth living, even if it means abandoning the very progeny you swore, through unspoken blood ties, to protect. This fear has engineered, in my mind, enough make-believe scenarios of my father's demise—cancer, heart disease, stroke—to cripple any anticipation of a happy future.

For each I've held an imaginary funeral. I've buried that man a thousand times. I've buried him in every thought of where I'd spread his ashes—across our national parks, the Bridger Range, our rivers that run through it all. In every trip I'll take to his headstone. In every silent curse I've sent his way for chewing tobacco all those years, for not drinking more water all his life, for eating processed food most of his meals. For never wearing a seat belt and driving too fast. For forgetting to take blood pressure medication even when his eyes begin to bulge. For thinking kale is for pussies and yoga for queers. For loving me too well and for making the unavoidable loss unbearable.

Because I've wanted to extend his life indefinitely, to stretch it like elastic across the timeline of eternity, and know that, if anything, my paternal cornerstone would be the one foothold I could always sink into—and brace off of—as I perpetually try to climb out of this horrific mental pit of torment I've dug for myself. Because, even though we've taken different paths, we share the same face, our uncanny resemblance.

I worry about my little brother, who was born fifteen years my junior, and how he might be robbed of the same parental guidance I've been given all these years. I worry about my own kids, unborn yet buried somewhere in my biological code, and how they might not get to know their grandfather. I think about what I'd say at his funeral—if I could say anything at all—and if it'd look anything like these stories I can't help but write. I fear the loss. The absence. But I also know, without being told, that he's feared my death just as much as I've feared his—every time he says *Be safe* or *I'm proud of you* before I leave town. Before I fly away. Because he doesn't want to live without me.

I know, without being told, that he's put me in a casket every time I've said goodbye. He's crafted just as many funeral speeches for me as I have for him, because, despite not understanding my brain disorder—my suicidal tendencies—he's come to respect the hardships of it all, knowing there've been days I've just barely survived. He cringes, as a dad is meant to, when I talk about wanting to die.

I think about it all, wrestling with a future loss I never want to face, and know only one thing for certain: I'll be taking ashes to the mountain peak Homer Young.

I'd just returned from Burning Man, a radical festival in the barren desert of northern Nevada, and felt wearied and worn from the experience. Despite this, I'd agreed to accompany my father on a multi-day camping trip with two other guys in the furniture industry.

The first night we'd camped near a little lake outside Wisdom, Montana. The range we traversed nestled directly in the continental divide; if I was to hike up to the southern precipice I'd be looking into Idaho. Crazy-ass Fred, a business tycoon in his seventies, had been out there many times before. Though now living in Washington, Fred still considers Montana his home, having fought wildfires in the state for decades and having been one of the danger-prone smoke jumpers for which Montana was once famous. Fred pointed to every surrounding summit expressing its prominence and elevation, but his finger kept moving back to one in particular. The highest. Homer Young.

The next morning I set the goal of going, inviting the crew, of whom only Fred opted out—he hiked to the adjacent divide. Bruce, Dean, and I headed directly toward Homer Young, no trail or topo map. We scrambled for miles along the rocky crag of the eastern ridge, making slow progress, making many complaints, and responding to Fred's frequent walkie-talkie broadcasts: "Bruce, you copy?"

"Go ahead, Fred."

"Got a visual on you."

"Okay . . ."

"Nowhere near the top."

"Great. *Thanks.*"

"Fred, out." This repeated every thirty minutes or so, until, of course, we were at the top—10,626 feet. We caught our breath, gazed below, and took photos, one of which is still a favorite: just me and pops and Homer Young.

On the way down, now welcoming the chore of easy breathing, we segued into those typical questions familiar to long hikes and distant road trips. Dean asked about Burning Man, curious about the sex and drugs affiliated with the event, but also inquired about other life goals of mine. I realized I'd never really asked my dad about his bucket list, if he had any regrets about becoming a family man so early, if he'd wished to have traveled more like me. I turned the questioning toward him. I thought numerous answers and reflections would pour from his mouth and mind; I thought I'd hear the sad lament of an unfulfilled vagabond's burden—*I wished I'd left Belgrade. I wished I'd seen the world.* But he gave only a single answer:

"I just wanna die before my kids do. I don't want to bury a child."

Some days I'm capable of making sense of the mess in my mind, but this is what I always come back to: we've been hardwired, as sentient beings, to avoid pain, to conserve energy, and to protect our progeny. But there's also early magic buried somewhere in our cells, giving a sick twist to this tragic miracle of consciousness. I shouldn't want to die, but I do.

But when gazing across the continuum of eternity I'm in no hurry to rob myself of the years I've been given. I've still got time to become something more, to create something worth sharing, and to show those I love that I'm going to be okay. That *we're* going to be okay. I'm tied to this life, this world, if, by anything, the blood in my veins. The blood we share. I can't die before my dad, not by my own volition, because if there's one thing worth fighting for it's to keep Bruce's bucket list alive, to avoid robbing him—my father, my friend—of the one goal he still hopes to achieve. I owe him that.

Staying alive hasn't been easy, but it's the daily gift I get to give. I look to my dad, my hero: I've buried that man a thousand times. He's buried me just the same. We'll bury each other a thousand more.

+

April's Fool
Sedona, Arizona

The water ran cold, as I'm sure it still does. A deluge of fire in my mind, that water. I had no intention of getting in, only there, at Slide Rock State Park, to watch the frigid snowmelt rush down the famous red rocks of Sedona, Arizona. It was April 1, 2011. A day set for fools.

We were a crew of five: Timmy, Jordan, Steve, Dale, and myself. All having our respective unspoken responsibilities—comedy, music, photography, rationality, navigation—but what's more, we had each other, at least for that weekend. Work had us stressed, had us needing that sweet fabricated freedom of travel. And it was this lure of adventure that wove us and drove us into the fiber of this country, 462 miles away from our home in San Diego to central Arizona.

With headlights dividing the darkness of the desert and camaraderie dispelling the melancholy of our minds, we spent our first night illegally camped behind the Sedona Dairy Queen. We awoke to a drier heat, to a sharper sunbeam. We awoke to a haphazard farmer's market taking place in the parking lot to which I'd entrusted my car while sleeping. The jewelry being displayed, turquoise and pewter, glistened in the rising sun, but our water-dependent bodies did not—the day had yet to make us sweat. The merchants—Apache, Hopi, I don't know—looked at us, confused or ashamed, as we staggered and crawled, one by one, from the ice-cream shop's cactus-riddled back lot, shirts abandoned, toothbrushes from mouths. *More matter out of place*, the Natives' eyes whispered. *More tourists to be trapped in this harsh terrain.*

High desert—scrub and sage, butte and barren brook, life waltzing so intimately with death. But Sedona was somehow different. Sedona offered red against green, earth against sky, bodies against dust. Even before knowing these nuances, choosing our destination came easy. Jordan grew up in Flagstaff, Sedona his backyard. He functioned as our deejay and guide, taking us straight to Bell Rock—a famous formation that Jordan's father had once summited. Progeny was now resolved—haunted—to do the same.

On that day, a day set for fools, Jordan attempted the climb; Steve and Dale followed but lagged behind in the certainty of a poor decision. Timmy and I remained at the base, discussing fragments of our lives we'd yet to divulge with one another. Living in different countries had hindered communication. We let memories wander from our lips and around the globe, from English pubs and apartments to the sacred soils of Israel and Palestine. We spoke of mutual friends, funerals, and failed relationships. My foolish words cooled the hanging heat as I spoke casually about people whom I loved and missed, of people who had moved away, and of people who had faded into withdrawn endeavors. Timmy wanted to know about John Kelly.

I think of John and remember Montreal, him grabbing my face and thanking me for the travels. I think of innocence and wonder: a tormented soul with a jovial spirit. I think of your quintessential Upstate New Yorker from Dobbs Ferry, all stereotypes fulfilled. I think of him being loud when brought to easy excitement, well-educated, and fraternal; it was hard not to love the guy, carrying himself in the manner of the entire *Good Will Hunting* rat pack, both in manifestation and mischief. The type of guy who would join any chant, regardless of purpose or content—hell, he started most of them himself. John agreed to nearly anything and, I'm pretty sure, spawned the original fear of missing out. He wanted to be at the center, believing it would hold.

I'd worked with him at Invisible Children, on the same traveling team, sharing a bunk bed when stationary at our communal San Diego living quarters—him, keeping me up at night by thinking every damn evening a slumber party to be celebrated. In the mornings he'd pull me aside, into the walk-in closet:

"Psst."

"What?"

"Come here."

"What?"

"Shut the door."

"*What?*"

"Do you think these are okay to wear to work?" A

pair of sweats.

"No."

"Really?"

"No."

"What about these?" Gym shorts.

"No. You got jeans or something? Khakis?"

Despite my advice he always looked like a high school gym coach: break-away pants, polo shirt, sneakers. My theory is that he held ready—and prayed for—a pick-up basketball game to start in the parking garage each afternoon.

John traveled with me on my first IC team, and, being the only two legal drivers in the group, we alternated the shared responsibility. He would miss turns while wailing to pop songs; he'd slap himself in the face to stay awake during those long stretches of Texas. We'd sprint across vacant parking lots, racing to no specified goal; we gave each other piggyback rides through the Boston Market. His goofiness infected. It spread.

John taught me important things, like how to extract value from the mundane—how to reevaluate life that was losing its luster due to unimaginative eyes. Finding this value came easy to John as he saw the world through a lens polished with childlike wonder. You wouldn't believe his renewed astonishment in each fleeting moment, a countenance of proof reflected in the van's windows as he stared at passing landscapes. For him, a California sunset never diminished in charm, a mountain range never in majesty. He taught me the benefits of folding a New York-style slice of pizza—still think of him when using the technique. But watching him eat, with each bite, it was almost like he *had* to fold the pizza. Like it wasn't a chosen act. And for him, it wasn't. What John taught me most about was Obsessive Compulsive Disorder.

"I need to tell you something," he said at lunch. "Could you not tell anyone?"

"Sure. Everything okay?"

"Well, we're leaving for the road in a week and I thought I should tell you—I have OCD."

"Okay? So what does that mean? Like, counting stuff? Does anyone at IC know?"

"Management knows. We've talked about it and they knew when they hired me. The whole thing is different than you'd expect. It's not always counting. I have what's called 'responsibility obsession.' I can't help but think that I—kill people."

"Kill people?"

"Say I open a newspaper and see that someone died in an accident, could be a total stranger, but I somehow find a way to blame myself—for not doing my rituals. And my fear, now, is that by going on the road I won't be able to control my compulsions in such an uncontrolled environment."

"So what do we do?"

"If I stay busy I should be fine, but I just wanted you to know."

"Sure. Thanks for telling me"—I put my arm around his shoulders—"We'll get through this just fine, I promise." Then again, I had no idea what he was up against.

I started noticing idiosyncrasies: he wouldn't wear certain colors on certain days, wouldn't shower before a specific hour, avoided crosswords. Wouldn't play particular people at ping-pong. Didn't like the number 7:47. It was cute. Endearing. The quirks endless. But can you imagine the haunt of thinking you were never careful, considerate, or thorough enough? Of thinking that any fatality or injury, in the news or otherwise, was your fault? Can you imagine such an abject state of guilt?

We'd encourage him, as his teammates, to alter the actions that perpetuated his daily torment—it was difficult to watch him suffer—but as we all know, even voluntary habits are hard to reverse after the concrete of conditioning has settled in our minds. *It's all about discipline*, he would say. *It's me versus myself.* Most days you'd never know he felt trapped and lost, living in fear. Most days you'd just have one hell of a good time with him.

Joining Invisible Children wasn't John's first attempt at distraction, or his only attempt at staying busy by helping others. He'd spent a semester studying in China, volunteered at various non-profits, and worked at a fish processing plant in Alaska. Nothing worked. Neither did Invisible Children. John went home early—back to New York—to get professional help for his OCD. I finished the tour and returned to San Diego to bleed out any remaining personal optimism I had for the world. My friendship with John then fell into that obscure category of people you plan to call but never do. We talked, at most, twice a year.

I told Timmy all this, some of which made John seem a fool, because these were the stories people wanted to hear—the ones I liked to tell—as they brought vivid color to an illness we knew nothing about. But John? He was no fool.

The reminiscing eventually reconvened in the present, Timmy and I finishing our lengthy fables and Jordan finishing his failed attempt to summit Bell Rock. He'd moved up the curve, abandoning the extremes, and was now stuck somewhere just short of the middle—a point where he couldn't go any higher, but couldn't safely get lower, life now waltzing intimately with death.

By the time Jordan inched his way down and extinguished his gut-rot feeling of impending doom, it was midday. The group then explored more of the region, basking on a rock formation referred to as the "muffin top," and ate sandwiches on a windy valley overlook. Steve snapped photos, one of which rests on my bedroom windowsill—the five of us, epic as ever. Brothers.

Our last stop of the day was Slide Rock State Park, a beautiful canyon illuminated by the setting sun that earned its title from a rock formation operating as a natural waterslide for anyone brave enough to enter the frigid stream. The slide had taken victims: rumors of fractured tailbones circulated.

Undeterred, we went to test the water by navigating trails, crossing bridges, and hopping along stepping stones. Then, the slide. But the water ran cold. So cold.

Despite growing up in Montana I've never enjoyed an arctic sting or carried winter in my blood. I've never been one to pursue water, even with my home's ample river runoffs carving out some of the best fly fishing terrain in the country. Evolved from the ocean, I've been slow to make my return.

I decide to forgo any slipping and sliding; Timmy followed suit to protect an already once-broken tailbone. Jordan, Steve, and Dale all performed the aquatic rite of passage, emerging soaked and rigid—no different from before, but changed. The departing sun offered little warmth to my buddies as they sought the drying desert heat that had long since vanished—a chilling breeze plagued the canyon. That's when I got a call—

"Tyler—"

"Anna, I can barely hear you. Reception's terrible."

"—have you—"

"I can't hear you, Anna."

"It—John—" Anna had traveled in the van with us.

"What?"

"I—don't—"

"Anna?"

"John—suicide, Tyler."

The final lesson John taught me is that life is a heavy burden when you have a heart of gold. Anna switched to texting: *How could this happen?* she kept asking. *How could this happen?*

I don't know, Anna.

But I do know. And I didn't have the heart to tell her that suicide happens when misery hits a fever pitch. That sometimes it just feels the best way out. The only solution. This was a man who'd been diagnosed with OCD since the seventh grade; a man who'd fought to survive till the age of twenty-four, just one week shy of his next birthday. This was a man, according to his journals, who didn't know how to sort his way through life. After countless hours of help, he'd concluded on one way to kill his OCD—and this wasn't his only attempt. First it was booze and pills. Then a hanging. Finally, a fatal dose of household chemicals turned into a poisonous cloud filling the confined space of his Jeep Liberty.

I took off my shirt. Pants, too. Walked over to Slide Rock and got in—muscles contracting, breath depleting. I moved with the flow of the forcing water, bobbing with the torrent as the icy liquid consumed me and crept into my lungs. I froze in every thought of John, in every apology I owed him: for not folding my pizza until I was in my mid-twenties, for not staying in better contact, for all the times I was rude to him on the road, but mostly for knowing that there was nothing any of us could have done to help him.

But there's one thing I could've done to ease the raging waters that coursed through his brain: I could have taken the journey with him, given him grace on the things I didn't understand, and been there at both his best and his worst—just as he was for the people that needed his help. I should've learned and listened. Should've dipped my toes in his watery chaos, tested the current, and took the plunge with him despite the temperature. I would've liked to have told him I was sorry, that I still am. I would've like to have taken back those stories I told earlier in the day— stories of a friend not yet known to be dead.

That night we camped in the towering pines of a dispersed camping site outside Flagstaff. It was cooler at that elevation, but the campfire warmed our tired bodies as flames turned the environment into a maze of silhouettes and unverifiable motion. Timmy spent the evening jumping the fire in his underwear. Jordan contemplated his near-death experience. Steve and Dale looked through photos of us, already feeding nostalgia. But on that day, April 1, 2011, there was only one person going home a fool. And there is still freezing water in my lungs. And I swear to God it still burns.

✛

IDENTIFYING FAMILY, GENUS, AND SPECIES

"Individual specimens and groups of specimens may have special significance."

—The National Park Service

✦

John Bond, Alien Hunter
San Diego, California

———————

He hasn't seen his brother in years. Thirty-seven years. Not sure if he's alive or dead, happy or healthy; nothing since their early twenties. Can you imagine? I can't. But I imagine you stop believing in God after thirty-seven years. After everything that happened. But he's reluctant to speak on it—religion, war, or otherwise. He just dreams of outer space.

We call him John Bond. Or John Player. Or King John. Just John on the darker days. You know the type: fossilized Asian janitor shuffling or scooting around the premises— this case, a natural history museum—near hunchbacked, near blind, resolving one hygienic disaster after the next, cart in tow: disinfectants, mops and brooms, the stuff you sprinkle on vomit, and, most commanding of all, a gray thirty-two-gallon garbage can with his name, "John," scrawled in black Sharpie.

His English is poor. Goofy as can be. You know the type. You've avoided him too.

I'm new to the place, been working here maybe a week—currently upstairs on the south register, right where no one wants to be—and in shuffles John, our first encounter, him pushing cart before the horse, moving from elevator to counter. I'm making failed attempts to flirt with my supervisor—the type of woman you'd want to marry; the type you'd want to come home to every night. The type, I imagine, who innately knows how to bake a perfect pie. Sweet as can be.

She likes me, too, I think, but she'd be damned to admit it. As my supervisor, my superior—in more ways than just professionally—we only *almost* flirt: her giving me books of poetry, me drawing her maps of the national parks on receipt paper.

It doesn't matter: John's giggling and ranting broken nonsense, interrupting. I can't tell if Lauren is bothered, in the style of old man accosting young woman, but she plays it cool when he hands her a dingy stuffed animal—a penguin. Found it somewhere during his daily travels: the theater, the room full of skulls, the California exhibit. It doesn't matter.

He giggles. Lauren smiles, laughs too, placing the plush in a drawer as John scoots toward the *Titanic* entrance. I'm dumbfounded, confused. What a bizarre exchange.

Next week, same thing. Upstairs, south side—where no one wants to be—with John, but no Lauren, and he's asking me about alien eyeballs, if I've found any, and I'm listening, confused.

"Oh, they are *so* good, Tyla." He can't pronounce my

name. "The alien eyeball, scrambled, and the alien jelly"—he rubs his meager pot belly. "I set traps"—he points like a child to the *Titanic* exhibit—"with toothpick and toothpaste." He giggles.

"That right, John?"

"John Bond, alien hunter. That's me. Like James Bond. I'm John Bond."

"John Bond, got it."

"You let John know, Tyla, if you see any—alien, okay?"

People avoid his company, flowing like water around stone—the path of least resistance. Few entertain his talk of eyeballs, the other janitors and security guards mostly calling him crazy without saying it. And I think this is typical to immigrants, punished in social circles and occupation for not knowing the common culture, for not speaking the conventional tongue. For talking nonsense. For cleaning toilets.

But damn he giggles. And little gets him down.

You know the type.

It's an interesting place to be employed, the museum. I'm hired under contractual obligation: for the museum to acquire the *Titanic* exhibit they first had to expand their work force to accommodate the required positions: additional service associates, someone at the green screen with a camera, two people renting and retrieving audio guides, one printing pictures with superimposed backdrops from the ship. The museum clambers and we become your crew: stoners, first-year undergrads, those who studied religion and work minimum wage to prove it (yours truly).

Over two hundred artifacts are present from the sunken ship: dinnerware, rivets, early twentieth-century garb. Rooms are reconstructed. A simulated iceberg lets you know just how cold that water was. To enter the exhibit, you pay extra. Considerably. Pictures are *not* allowed.

Tragedy, it seems, one-hundred years prior, has landed me a job. Fitting.

The days are what you'd expect: tickets—lots of tickets—and content customers, all excited to re-live the nautical nightmare, except for the random few, of course, that ruin your day with poor manners and rude discourse. My nightmare.

I smile. Nod. Become the buffoon these insulting customers believe me to be. I sell memberships. Talk about the Foucault pendulum in the foyer. The megalodon hanging from the ceiling. Sometimes I get stationed in the theater, which is easy, and gives me time to read—Cormac McCarthy mostly—in the closet alongside tubs of 3-D glasses.

Nights are different: sometimes we throw paper airplanes off the top floor, four stories, and they swirl and twirl downward, crashing near the allosaurus. Sometimes it's bouncy balls. The lights, on timers, shut off. Doors lock. Silence, eerie and still, ensues. Nothing comes alive, though we are asked this daily—nothing except our imaginations: bones waltz in the shadows. Aliens, plausibly, lurking nearby.

Everyone is younger. And I feel old. I feel a failure. This is strikingly apparent when a mandatory meeting is called to discuss how smoking pot is not allowed on our fifteen-minute breaks. Seems a given. But alas, I'm on the outer cusp, a generational misfit.

Despite this, I linger for longer than a year, making the Visitor Service Associate cut when the *Titanic* leaves, a traveling exhibit off to another locale. I, too, segue, moving from VSA to special events, helping with high school proms, Yelp events, Qualcomm fundraisers. By then I'm pseudo-dating a co-worker, but not the one worth marrying. We kiss in elevators, the only place without security cameras; we sneak on the roof at twilight to overlook the city; we fool around in my car at shift's end.

But it is John, despite the artifacts and late-night mischief and love affairs, that shimmers in my mind. It is John, a living exhibit to our humanity, that I will never forget.

He doesn't just eat eyeballs; there are other things. Like dinosaur meat—*where do you think the bones come from*, he says, pointing, again, like a child into *Fossil Mysteries*. And eighty-billion-year-old duck eggs. And hundreds of pounds of whale blubber. He giggles. He tells me he'll eat *anything*.

There are girlfriends, too. He goes to other planets to find them, specifically a place called Goldilocks. The first lasts a week, but they break up as she makes him do too many jumping jacks. The next one lasts maybe a week longer and is abandoned because she is eating all the palm trees of Southern California. Another drinks too much of the already diminishing lake water. There are many others, all with their quirks. None last long and sometimes, oddly, John seems lonely in his fictional losses. He tells me to call him "John Player" when he is dating.

The cart, he claims—with disinfectants, mops and brooms, stuff you sprinkle on vomit—is his spaceship to other worlds.

"Find any aliens last night, John?" I can't help but provoke.

"No, Tyla, I stayed up *all* night hunting—toothpicks and toothpaste. Slept in the"—he points to the *Titanic* entrance. "In the—"

"Did you sleep in the replica cabin, John?" I ask. He giggles.

"Oh, John is *so* silly, Tyla. Just a crazy old man. Don't believe anything I say." He giggles. He scoots. He pushes his cart, that simple name scrawled across the garbage can.

You know the type: palpably kind, uplifting, supernatural yet ordinary. Gentle. Innocent. The type you hope will be working the same shifts as you. The type you wish you'd met somewhere other than work. The type you'd take as a grandpa or a brother or, at worst, a best friend. The type that makes you forget you're depressed, and self-loathing, and suicidal.

I hope you know the type.

Months pass, friendships further develop, paper airplanes swirl and fall. Elevator kissing persists. And then lightning.

South desk—where no one wants to be—and we're discussing our former lives: Diana missing summers with the National Park Service, Brian lamenting the better pay of dealing drugs, and me longing for the storms over southern Florida.

John giggles—didn't see him there, cart and all—and he misses lightning too. He misses home.

The transition is seamless, the way our conversation somehow shifts from lightning and thunder to memories of mass murder and human brutality, as if the connection is obvious and organic. Something's triggered.

His countenance changes with ominous thoughts gathering like a thunderhead: clear skies to broken smiles, gentle eyes to overcast sorrow. He speaks of death camps; he speaks of genocide. "I am from Cambodia," he says, and shuffles towards the *Titanic* entrance. He's not giggling anymore.

The Cambodian genocide, from 1975 to 1979, though referenced less in America than other modern atrocities, proved as awful as many of those we could more easily call to mind. But why contrast violations of human rights? Heinous is heinous. Dreadful is dreadful.

During this era of confused civil war, with the dictator Pol Pot instituting a Maoist dictatorship through the use of an organization called the Khmer Rouge, more than twenty percent of the population was murdered. Twenty percent. An estimated one and a half to three million people.

Can you imagine? I can't.

Educated people were targeted first, especially those wearing glasses or knowing a foreign language. The upper-class got annihilated. The peasantry was divided, displaced, starved, and shuffled from one labor camp to the next, from one killing field to the next. Rape became rampant, murder a casual activity. And the more I research it, the less I seem to understand—how human violence reaches a fever pitch; how things of nightmares break the astral plane, permeating the waking life, turning actions to savagery and vice. John helps me imagine.

"I was sent to a labor camp"—this information comes slowly from day to day, week to week, month to month; he's open to talk, eager, though it pains him—"in a rice paddy, sometimes in the jungle, for nearly three years, working all day. They gave us half cup of rice a day. I was starving. So skinny"—he pats his meager pot belly—"you wouldn't believe it now!" A slight giggle. "So, secretly, like this"—he mock eats something—"I ate maggot to stay alive. If they had caught me, with maggot—POW!"—mock gunfire—"they would have killed me. On the spot. It's no good, Tyla. No good. Of the thirty in my work camp, two survived. Just two."

"Jesus, John . . ." I whisper.

"Why do you think I joke about food? Why do you think I talk about alien eyeball? I lived off maggot for years, Tyla. I ate trash. And I saw people, the wealthy, trading gold watches for can of beans. This, all this"—he insinuates, with his hands, the material world—"it means nothing when you're starving. I joke because I have starved. I understand the absurdity." His eyes well. Mine too.

"I've seen—" he tries to continue. "I've seen . . . they'd force us into theaters, Tyla. They made us watch execution, over and over. They'd slit throats like this"—more gestures, this time with the suggestion of blood spraying—"all over us in the crowd. And they'd hit others in the back of the head, with a bolt; blood would come out the mouth, the ear, the eye.

"It's no good, Tyla. No good." And he shuffles, off to clean something. "Bye, Tyla. See you tomorrow."

"See ya, John Bond."

"No, Tyla, not today. Today I'm just John."

More and more it seems he is just John. Less giggling. More and more somber. More reserved. There are times I ask him to dinner. And I wish in those moments that I innately knew how to bake the perfect pie, sweet as can be, to say: there is beauty in this life, there is *good* in us, somewhere, somehow, and that I am sorry. That I'm really sorry.

He refuses—not the apology, which I never give with words, but the invitation—saying he can't leave his house other than for work; that it's too difficult. He stays at home, instead, and watches *Tom and Jerry*, though he doesn't actually know the name of the show: *cat and mouse, like this*, he gestures.

I ask him other things: "What's your given name, John?"

He giggles. "You'd be embarrassed for me if I told you! I used to be upper class. Now I clean toilets!" He giggles. "But a king is still a king, and I am king of the toilets! Call me King John today!" I giggle. And bow.

I ask him how he made it to the States, to which he says, during a Vietnamese attack, he escaped the labor camp, walked through multiple minefields, hundreds of miles, sleeping half submerged in rivers along the way to avoid getting captured, to Thailand and gained refugee status. He then had the choice to relocate to various countries, and, speaking four different languages, he felt comfortable with his choices. So he came to America, working as a cab driver, then a convenience store clerk, and now this, a janitor.

In the midst of these transitions, a well-to-do, affluent family—that of a state senator, I think John said—took him in, offering him a new home, but John didn't like the comfort; didn't like being waited on and not doing his own laundry. So he left.

60 Minutes, later on, asked to cover John's story, but he was too self-conscious about his English to agree. He now lives alone. Unknown. Somewhere buried in the forgotten districts of San Diego. You know the type.

I ask him his age. He giggles. He doesn't know. I ask about his own family: "Never found out what happened to them, if they're alive or dead. Never heard from them again after we were separated and I was sent to work camp. It's been thirty-seven years. I had a daughter. A brother.

"I still look, Tyla, saving my money and taking trips back every—maybe five or ten years. I spend all my money on calling cards, calling Cambodians that might know something. I'm closer than ever because I've located my brother's ex-wife. She might know something. I just"—his eyes well—"I just . . . if I could somehow get back, just one more time, I think I'd find him." And I don't know what to say, unable to imagine such a loss, so he shifts the questioning to me. "Why do you think I joke about outer space?" he asks.

"I don't know . . ." I can't think about space. I'm thinking about his life, the endless search. Futile. Lonely in the things he's lost, the horrors he's seen. The endless search. Thirty-seven years. I'm thinking how today he is just John. How I am just Tyler. And how we are just humans cleaning toilets and selling museum tickets and sharing secret stories about secret lives.

"Because, Tyla, it's the only place I know—where there is no war."

His health is failing and, as he tells me, there is tension between him and a new custodian. John's stressed out and disheartened. He's losing vision in one eye. His stomach—the one that once starved him to near death—it hurts. And I know he knows he's dying, but we don't talk about it. Instead we discuss aliens. And eyeballs. And Goldilocks.

He can't afford both medical treatment and searching for his family. So he chooses the latter. He tells me he wants to go home without saying it. He tells me, without saying a word, that he wants to die looking for those he once loved.

No, he doesn't say it, he just giggles that giggle, pushing his cart off to another planet, to a place where there is no war; where he can't be reminded that even *Tom and Jerry* cartoon violence derives from something—from actuality, perceptibility, a mistreatment that is only funny between an imaginary cat and mouse. A mistreatment that is all too real. So he time travels in retrograde, inwards and backwards, thirty-seven years, to a place where gold watches don't buy cans of beans; to a place where maggots don't save lives; to a place where daughters still have fathers and brothers are still brothers. No work camps. No starvation. No killing fields.

In all his travels, outer space or otherwise, I know John must have learned the secrets to this universe because, somehow, still, he giggles. And it rings truer than anything I've ever heard.

So I start a secret fundraiser. And we—the stoners, the first-year undergrads, the ones who studied religion and work minimum wage to prove it—raise enough money to send John home. The day I write the check I search the museum up and down—looking for the obscure little Asian man—questioning personnel and being sent from one exhibit to the next, security guards bothered that I'd willingly seek out the man who rants broken nonsense about aliens.

I find him cleaning a toilet, down in the horse exhibit, and hand him the slip of paper. He looks at it, confused. "We want you to go find your brother, John."

Tears stream. He holds me, shaking. And says thank you without saying it.

A date is set, a one-way ticket bought, and he resigns from the museum. The night before he departs I boil eggs; I make a trip to the grocery store. I then awake and go to his house, for the first time, to give him a ride to the airport. His bags are packed, two in total, his entire life contained; we take pictures outside while the neighborhood kids skateboard circles around us. He giggles.

In the car John asks what kind of music I like. "My

favorite song," he says, "is 'Girls Just Want Fun' by Cindy Laupa."

At the terminal, while unloading, I hand him a paper bag. Inside are toothpicks, toothpaste, and hardboiled eggs painted like alien eyeballs. He holds them up as if they are his own eyeballs. He giggles, but I see tears, behind these new eyes, sneaking down. It's a gentler form of letting go than I'm used to. I'm saying goodbye again—right where no one wants to be—to a friend not passing away but simply passing on. Chasing a hope. Looking for a family he will never find. A family most likely thirty-seven years deceased. And I know I'll never see John Bond, or John Player, or King John, or just John again. That I'll never know the type again.

"Thank you, Tyla."

"Be careful out there, John"—I'm crying, too—"and if you come across any aliens, use the toothpaste and toothpicks, all right?" He gives one last giggle.

Months later, I'm walking home from the grocery store, hands to elbow nooks in cumbersome sacks: vegetables for my smoothie kick, cereal and almond milk, Top Ramen. My pocket's vibrating but I don't care. It goes to voicemail—a random number from New Jersey. I listen later, wishing, more than anything, I had answered the call because it never comes again:

"Hi, Tyla. Hi, Tyla. I wanted to say thank you to you. Without you I couldn't have made it. There is a great thanks from the bottom of my heart. I haven't called because some villages . . . lots of place in Cambodia don't have electricity. And I don't have phone, either.

"And, um, I wanted to tell you . . . about my brother. I just wanted to tell you. I found him, Tyla. I'm so happy. I found him—I found my brother."

I've called the number back a couple of times—no answer. And I've replayed that voice message a dozen times, crying with each listen. I miss John—I miss him, looking to outer space and giggling, knowing he's out there. Somewhere. Galaxy hopping, his brother now in tow. Across the better cosmos. The only place where there is no war.

+

A Brother Divided

Bozeman, Montana

For the next five months I'll find myself in a strange mathematical circumstance involving my little brother, something that will never happen again in our lives. That is, he is currently half my age: thirty versus fifteen.

He came as a surprise, a late addition to the same core family of which I was born: Bruce, Loretta, Treaver, Tyler. And now a fifth: Troy. I first heard of his creation—his existence in utero—at a furniture convention in Bozeman, Montana, at a GranTree Inn, with my older brother and me sitting on one queen bed, my parents across the room on another. The short distance between the beds felt like a moat, a fissure, keeping my once-safe reality from the hard truth that was about to come mess it up.

I thought my parents were getting a divorce, and I

had had all day to contemplate what such a family vivisection would look like. With whom would I live? Which parent would have to quit the family business? My mother's continuous tears suggested such a division, my father's restlessness the same. They waited until that evening, after the board meetings and buffet-style banquet, to make us savvy to the actuality: a pregnancy, an addition, a little brother. Troy.

He's now the same age I was when he was born. After all of the diapers, the babysitting, the piggyback rides, the hide and seek—he is now that same age. No longer an idea, no longer a kid, but becoming a man. This is odd for me because, looking at the entirety of his existence—a pregnant and shared mother, a childhood, the here and now—the next few years will be the formative ones of his life.

He didn't know me when I faced such a transition. But I have seen his every single day—his birth, first steps, maturation. This is not a situation brothers often find themselves in, a rift in fraternal time. But I think of us now, a divisible difference of two, and wonder what this suggests. Because if you were to divide me by any means—physical, mental, emotional, spiritual—you wouldn't find two of him as the result. He already usurps all the parts of my whole.

If you were to divide me in the way my father taught me to gut a deer, this would be the result: incision from sternum to crotch with an ever mindful consideration of the entrails. Then, slowly, unfolding the insides to the out—revealing not organs and blood, but dirt and foliage—an internal landscape as rugged as the Rockies would emerge. Mountains would rise from my spine like a dividing line between my struggles—a schism dictating the path of least resistance, one vertebrae after another. Each summit with the runoff of thirty long winters, melting to the meadows below. I'd tell my brother that life moves in seasons. I would then take his fingers and press them to each river, stream, and creek, and watch his face light up as he first finds the pulse.

As my body keeps unfolding, like the beginnings of an exposed planet, saplings of abundant varieties—pine, fir, bristlecone, oak, elm, aspen, olive—would sprout in the representation of every friend I've made, of all the people who have crossed my path. Some would grow together from communal roots, while others would rise above the rest. Some would be caught in accidental fires. Others burned with intention.

I would tell him to listen to the wind and the wolves as they howl, to patiently await the rattle of the bamboo stalks that have grown—all their lives—with the dream of finally being tall enough to reach each other. I would want him to look for patterns—in the soil, in the stars, but mostly in himself. To learn that it's the unknown complexities that make this life so simple—like a cherry blossom, and how it can bear fruit. To drink more water, to stand up straight, to recognize that the middle of nowhere is always the beginning of somewhere. That despite what he might be shown and experience, to trust that humans are inherently good.

I'd tell him that with autonomy comes responsibility. With freedom of speech a necessity to listen. With stewardship the obligation to kindness. That if ever distraught, to chase new experiences and let state boundaries form the fault lines of a broken heart starting to heal: cardiac ranges, like mountains, where the plates grind and bind back together. To see the world and dwell in its obscurity, but to also tread softly—to demand less, not more.

I would offer my tangled web of trails and invite my brother to walk each one—some easy loops in the foothills, others strenuous forays into the backcountry; I would encourage bringing bear spray and keeping it accessible as the most dire of beasts always defend the subconscious.

I could tell him that in those first fifteen years my biggest fear was that he would end up like me—not in manner, or temperament, or worldview—but in depression. I would tell him, on those dreary days when life seems unworthy of further attempt, to find that pulse again, to put his hands back in the dirt, and to reconnect with the rhythm of the earth. To never leave us.

I would tell him that the human heart is just an organ and that, though capable of love, it is not to be celebrated beyond the rest of the body. I would implore learning to love from all available sources—the eyes, the ears, the skin, the tongue—and that every action carries karmic value, whether good, bad, or indifferent. I would say to be intentional.

Moving further along the trails, he would find a history of keeping goals like promises and some tough lessons in being alone; a history of handwritten letters and an attempt at letting others in—giving people a chance. That is what the wooden signposts would say at each mile marker: *Let others be a part of this journey with you.*

I would tell him to be slow to anger, but to never quell emotions, because they develop for a reason. I would say: Don't shut your mind down as a defense, not against pain or loss, because it will bear long-term damage that is difficult to recover from. I would say it's okay to hurt.

I would tell him that most of the battles he is going to face in this life are going to be faced alone. And most of them will be losing. I would confess that every human heart has a divisible line of conflict, that war is messy, and that there will always be casualties. But whatever remains, whatever survives, he must give it to someone—his friends, his family, a lover—because that will become his only true home.

I would tell him to honor every person he loves by loving what he does. To create. To fight for the betterment of something. Because no one likes to witness wallowing or wasted talent. Because the best thing he can do for the people he loves is to try; the worst thing is to be apathetic, lazy, and overly ironic. I'd say: Love the things you love and others will love you for it. It's that simple. And finally, I'd tell him to be honest—no matter how painful.

I wasn't sure if I was going to make it, to see him grow. But I'm here—thriving—and can now tell him all of these things, hoping they will resonate in some way—

But I won't.

I look to my little brother and feel so much pride. He came as a surprise, as a fissure between my life as the youngest child and that of the middle. And he has surprised me every day since. Now I want *him* to be surprised.

I will let him learn the same way I did: by exploring these landscapes, both internal and external. By letting people unfold before him, into their own orbs of endless adventure, and to take each unfolding as a gift. Origami. Even with all the paper cuts. That is the best I can do as a brother twice his age. A brother divided.

+

Red Mountain
Clarkston, Montana

Chad is the first one cursed with the fervor, heart-tinder freshly aflame. "Can we burn that to the ground?" he asks, pointing to my uncle's camper. I squint through a deepening haze of dusk, eyes blurring to the change of wind now blowing bonfire in my direction. I squint toward my inquisitor, his wayward thinking contagious: I don't know Chad well but like where his head is at. I turn to Unc Donnie, the owner of the property in question, and casually repeat Chad's words.

Unc muses a moment, now distracted from his alcohol-induced fireside ramblings, now silently running a hand over his graying goatee. Flame illuminates our leader: jean shorts rest a half-foot lower than respectable, forced down by a bulging belly chock-full of diabetes; the bulge itself is feebly covered by some thrift store T-shirt inadequate in size and celebrating a high school Donnie did not attend. His skin suggests years of outdoor blue-collar abuse. Missing teeth suggest the same—but of a much darker source than the sun. The former addict muses. He muses and stands to walk away. "Let me get the kerosene," is all he says.

Arson wasn't the plan when we drove to the Montana countryside that afternoon—myself and six other ruffians. We just wanted to be there, in the wild, together. The destination, Red Mountain, was sacred in our eyes—

Red Mountain, we whisper when we are away.

Red Mountain, we say when the uninformed ask.

Red Mountain, Red Mountain, we pray when we need our demons at bay.

And it whispers back, the mountain itself, begging us come home.

We listen, we heed the call, and come marching back, dressed in the skin of accountants, teachers, students, day laborers, and full-time volunteers. Not everyone is acquainted, but this doesn't matter, not on the mountain. Because for the bohemian type, such as Unc Donnie, this place is serenity. For the rest of us, an escape.

My older brother, Treaver, and his best friend, Chad, spend their days preoccupied with careers and families. Rusty fosters and festers the stress of applying to medical school, Dan is home on break from language studies in Russia, and Space Brad is feeling lost in the anxiety-ridden doldrums of not having direction. I'm lost too, just coming off my second tour with Invisible Children and only having exhaustion to show for it—employers, it turns out, are far less interested in altruistic accolades than I'd anticipated.

Going to Red Mountain means a break from it all. The only requirement is an invitation and an initiation—an initiation which comes at the summit after a disorienting drive into agricultural backcountry: interstate to city road; city road to river bridge; river bridge to dirt passage. With each off-road bend and twist, mirroring an adjacent stream, reality is rattled—or, maybe, just redefined—through the plume of dust.

By the time we reach the top nothing matters but the view: an overlook of valleys and meadows painted by Apollo himself—the sun casting gold across the winter wheat. It is here, with the divine, that a new visitor to the mountain raises an unclean shot glass—which has remained half-buried in the dirt since our last visit—full of Drambuie to his or her lips, consumes, and then chases it with a shot of creamer.

We grimace and laugh, a rite of passage complete. The mountain rejoices. Another new believer.

The empty alcohol bottles are then placed ceremoniously on the Drambuie Tree, the hardy skeleton of a once-lively evergreen. This sun-bleached idol, now skewering and sprouting dozens of brown glass jugs as if blossoms, is best photographed as a silhouette against the sunset. From this vantage, on the southern slope, you come to understand the lay of the land—the dry, barren vegetation that buries thistles deep into your socks; the sprouting patches of crimson shale giving the place its branding—

Red Mountain, Red Mountain, we pray when we need our demons away.

There are other colors as well: ocean blue in the sky, gilded grass on the ground. Shining debris peppers the terrain—broken window panes, disconnected Jacuzzi tubs, boxes of china plates—anything my uncle can salvage from local thrift store filth. We take baseball bats to it all. We wield hammers and golf clubs. It peppers the land.

From this vantage you see down the rolling crevasses, onto other people's property and into their settlements. These are the junkyard lives of hermits avoiding the government—Clapper will draw a gun if you approach. Pen-Pen will only ask for meth. Both are alarming and intriguing for different reasons, both elusive as mountain lions.

They talk to the land, Clapper and Pen-Pen. They hear it whisper, too.

This is what makes the mountain mythology, both pre- and post-visit. This is what I keep to myself, the fables I know others wouldn't want to hear. *White trash*, they might say. *Redneck*. But while we are here, for these fleeting moments, I assure you, the mountain is alive.

Donnie removes a bluebird's nest from his makeshift camper; the rest is smothered with kerosene. Thoughts become flammable. Creed turns occult. Energy surges from our hearts and minds. To think everything began so normal, everything peaceful until Chad's meandering thoughts turned to fire—scalding his tongue with one simple query: *May we please burn?*

Before I realize it, we're circled around Unc's mountain camper, roman candles in hand. We light the fuses, aiming the candles at the open windows and door. Orbs of illumination rocket from each participant, briefly exposing devilish grins of delight. Everyone thirsts to be the igniter—

My dear mountain, I whisper down, *what have we done?*—

A flaming ball whizzes past my head, then another. I crouch, firing back. It's a war zone, and the emergency is rising up inside of me, especially after Dan, the piece of shit, wins the unspoken competition. With one well-placed shot the camper becomes an inferno. Upholstery disintegrates, metal framing twists and withers, wood blackens to soot. There is an explosion. Those close enough recoil from the pressure and heat. I drop my camera, falling to the ground.

"Forgot to remove the propane tank," Donnie chuckles. We chuckle, too—

I'm back up, on my feet, and screaming in Rusty's face. I scream like a child born of bloodshed, full on, in his face. And I want to kill, I want my claws in his throat—

He screams back. And I'm afraid of what I see. What I feel. Because I'm starting to understand this fire's inside me. Inside him. And I want everything to burn.

We rub ash under our eyes. We inhale fumes, toxic, and shirts are coming off—

Space Brad is rolling a flaming tire at Chad—

Dan is throwing firecrackers at me—

Rusty is in the fire, glowing like a fucking god, but he is not consumed—

FUCK. Where's Treaver? Where's Donnie? I only see shadows dancing on the other side of the darkness. And then I know they are here. Somehow they found me. My demons—

The mountain whispers up, *Are you happy yet?* But I am not happy. I am not. Because we have not yet burned everything. I'm not done, not yet. I won't go back to the haunt of being alive, to the haunt of heavy skin sagging from my spoiled meat, not yet. I won't. So I burn it all. I burn my fading confidence in the human species. I burn every day I've ever woken up and wished, yearned, to be dead. I burn it—the feeling of rodents trapped in my skull, scratching, frantic to get out. The inadequacies. The self-doubt. The desire to die. I burn it all.

Are you happy yet? But I am not. I am not. I remove every shattered dream from my head and place the pieces before me. Because I thought I could make a difference, I thought I could be good—at something, at anything—I thought I could help in some small way. I thought—I don't know what I thought. So I piss on it all, spit in disgust, kick the soiled thoughts into the blaze. *FUCK.* I watch my wasted hopes cackle and fizz, cry out, beg for mercy, but they won't find it here. Oh no, not anymore. I let them burn.

Are you happy yet? But I am not. There is more. So I collect every face I've ever seen and turn them back to dust—no, fuck dust, this is ash, an eternal cremation—and I watch all the soot and bullshit billow up and blow away in the wind. I need everyone dead. I need every single possible future loss. I need it now, on my terms. *Now*, not later. So I burn them all. And I start pulling the rodents from my brain, one at a time: fuck you terrorism, disease, murder; fuck you suicide, depression, drowning; fuck you hope, optimism, and trying to cope; fuck you—*everybody* and *everything*. I burn it all: my mom, my dad, my brothers; I burn every person I've ever fought for, ever tried to help; I burn every friend I've ever loved and then shit on with indifference. I kill them. And I won't stop until I have nothing left to burn. Not until this heavy flesh has melted down to bone and everyone I know is buried, away, gone. Maggots, flies, and rot. I need them dead. I need that promise of pain, of loss—I need it over with. I need it over with. God, please, I just need this over with—

Tears run black with ash. I taste it on my tongue, streaking down my cheeks, into my mouth, and am reminded of the distinct flavor of hell that this world can put you through. My blood runs thick like tar. Crows circle. It smells like burning hair, and I am singeing! I'm on fire! I'm on fucking fire!—

Have I made you happy yet? the mountain begs. And I am screaming back, amongst the flames, a glowing god, burnt but not consumed. And for a moment I'm not haunted. For a moment I'm not scared. Because I am beginning to understand I am more than my depression. I am more than my losses. I am more than the regrets I never rectified, the shame I never stamped out, the goodbyes I never gave. That all life *doesn't* have to be suffering. I am beginning to understand.

Donnie's camper is reduced to a ring of ash, the kitchen sink, and a piece of the fridge. The earth twinkles with dying embers, a mirror to the stars, as lunacy abates. The hangover to demolition sets in with a strange growing concern over the power Prometheus gifted us so long ago. We now know why the gods refused to share. It's just too much for us to handle.

We awake the next morning with the return of the sun. Groggy and dazed, we halfheartedly mill about, remembering the previous night as a collective dream. We gather what is salvageable and drive from dirt passage to river bridge, river bridge to city road, city road to interstate. Reality restores. Time becomes measurable. Responsibility resurfaces. Jobs, families, finances. Chad is once again my older brother's best friend, my older brother just a brother.

They both go on to have more kids, becoming again, as they always were, great fathers. Rusty gets into med school, Dan becomes a lawyer, Space Brad finds his purpose in philosophy and herbalism. Everyone grows, like vegetation returning stronger after a vicious burn, nourished by the fertile land. Fireweed, they call it, and it can paint an entire hillside pink with the hope of restoration.

We start cleaning the place up, removing trash, building a cabin. But we're never all gathered together again in the same place at the same time. I eventually put my skin back on, embracing those things lingering in the deepest corners of my darkness, things yet named, things that can't be named. Because not everything burns. I start writing more, still haunted, but with better ways to purge—or so I think. I write, putting pain to page.

Because I am pink with the spring.

Across an entire hillside.

Restoration.

And this, I praise the mountain, I am starting to understand.

+

RESTORATION

"Although a standard dictionary defines restoration as returning something to a former or unimpaired condition, the NPS's use of the term natural system restoration recognizes that reaching the former or unimpaired condition may take many years to decades."

—The National Park Service

+

Babel
Raleigh, North Carolina

It began with the drying rack. I was putting piled dishes away twice daily, leading me to think no one else was helping in the chore. So I stopped, without warning, to prove the obvious truth. I watched as half-moist dinner plates stacked on dry cutting boards, half-melted spatulas propped still-oily frying pans, and blackened cookie sheets hung from dull cutlery. The structure grew into an unstable Tower of Babel, stretching to the heavens as if *uncleanliness* was actually next to godliness.

Drinking glasses disappeared from cabinets and the silverware holder became as empty as my belief that anything would ever change—the drying rack now our only means of culinary storage. The disorganization occasionally deterred me from eating, but I held strong over putting just one dish away. A point had to be made.

Two weeks passed before Steve caved, but only after our largest mixing bowl toppled from the height of the tower and shattered inside the garbage disposal. Such a display of disorder couldn't be ignored. Plates moved back to cupboards, silverware to drawers.

I was brushing my teeth when the salvation came, my ears perking to the sweet sounds of restoration. I emerged from the bathroom to an empty rack, to a domestic heartbeat restored. Despite Steve's actions, though, the other roommate, Alex, could've built in perpetuity.

The next experiment regarded toilet paper. Our bulk Costco pack had run out, so I made the desperate purchase of a smaller pack of six. Gone in a week. Bought another. Vanished, too. It seemed like we were always in need of more—a ship in the process of sinking—yet no one noticed. So I took two spare rolls and stashed them in my room. I bet on who'd take the initiative first, especially after the last communal roll was reduced to cardboard tubing.

Two days passed, yet the tube remained. No one seemed panicked. So I fled.

I fled to North Carolina to visit my family, my parents in the Tar Heel State from Montana to attend a furniture convention. I tagged along, claiming five days of freedom from uncleanliness. I was 2,455 miles from Babel—from my squalor in San Diego—staying in a hotel of unsoiled dishes and replenished toiletries. No language barrier, nothing lost in translation.

This proved the therapy I needed, free of a city which I no longer considered home: San Diego; visiting family who wanted nothing more than to see me come back home: Montana; and exploring the only place I felt at home anymore: nature. I studied the trees—swamp tupelo and bald cypress—while my parents sampled sofas and settees. The trip wasn't entirely a vacation though. I went to visit another family, too: the Henns.

I hadn't seen Nate's parents, Bob and Julie, since his funeral almost three years prior. Hadn't kept in touch. He was their son and my best friend, but we were now on opposite sides of a missing mutual connection. Little bound us together. It felt strange driving the two hours to their house, especially considering I'd once contemplated living with them—Nate had begged me to move in after my time at the chateau had ended.

The day before I made the drive, furniture-market friends complimented me on the nice thing I was doing, visiting the Henns. What they didn't know, though, was how my motives were selfish. I wanted to *feel* that connection to Nate again—just wanted to feel something again. Untreated depression had spoiled any emotion left in my heart.

I called when I got close, confused on the location. "Bob's Pizza Parlor, how can I help you."

"I'm sorry, I must have the wrong number."

"I'm messing with you. This is Bob Henn!"

"Oh, hey! It's Tyler, I've been emailing with Julie about coming to visit today. You still free?"

"Of course, Tyler! How close are you? Let me get you some directions. Finding our house can be a bit of a nightmare." He wasn't lying. I circled the area several times, navigating three separate roads with damn near identical names, only to find their house buried in the thick of the countryside. I knocked somewhat timid, nervous, but was welcomed with cheer.

"Water?" Bob asked, already pouring it.

"That'd be great, thank you."

"Let me tell you, we got this reverse osmosis system—had it installed years ago—and let me tell you, it takes the impurities right out of the water—or desalinizes—wait, I can't—"

"Bob! He doesn't want to hear *that* right now! Geesh!" This was Julie, squeezing her husband's arm, smiling at me. "Come on, Tyler. Have a seat." I felt at home, fears dissipating. It was funny to think that I'd worried so much over what they'd be like. Depressing to think my only other impression of them had come at the height of abject sorrow: a son taken by the unbelievable, and inconceivable, reality of terrorism. Their characteristics shone through: generous, playful, perceptive.

"Didn't you have your first Philly cheesesteak with Nate? While you were still a vegetarian?"

"I forgot about that! Yeah, it was my first time in Philadelphia—I kinda thought I had to!"

"He got such a kick out of that."

"Seems like you guys remember more about my time on the road than I do."

"Nate talked about you a lot. Told a lot of stories. He cherished your time together." The comment hurt, as pleasant things do when people are dead, taking me back to the funeral—

During the service, Nate's sister asked if I wanted to spend time in the family room, away from the throng of grieving visitors, because Julie wanted to finally meet me. I agreed, only to find myself wrapped tight in her embrace. No "Hello." No "Nice to meet you." Just this: "I've wanted to thank you. Nate told me you were one of the reasons he came back to his faith, that his conversations with you in the van inspired him to believe again—you have no idea what kind of relief that brings at a time like this. Thank you, Tyler."

The rest of my time in the family room found me defending my non-Christian values to Nate's zealous grandma who lamented the damnation of my soul. Uncomfortable yet funny. But always, from the corner of my eye sat Bob. Not talking. Not functioning. And never in my life have I seen a man so broken—

"What else have you been up to?" Julie asked, pulling me back to the present. "What've you been doing the last couple years?"

"Did you know I've been trying to visit all the national parks?"

"No, what a goal! How many have you been to?"

"I'm going to Congaree tomorrow. It's gonna be number thirty-eight of the fifty-nine."

"What've been your favorites?"

"Yellowstone and Rocky Mountain are special places to me—I've spent the most time in those ones—but there are so many great parks. I visited the two in Hawaii a little over a year ago. I really loved it out there."

"Oh, you've *got* to hear Bob's Hawaii story."

Bob, on cue, launched into recounting a multi-day hike across Kauai. "We're out on this trail, right—this is years ago, I was much younger then—just me and a couple guys, and this place is remote, three days from civilization, walking these magnificent cliffs where they filmed those epic shots in *Jurassic Park*. But my foot gets infected, this really nasty type of foot rot, and I can barely walk, right, and there's no hope of me getting back to the car—I mean, this infection could've killed me! We have no idea what we're gonna do, so we just start walking, and what do we come upon— a completely naked guy. Stark naked! Out in the middle of nowhere! And, get this: he's a medical doctor. Just some weirdo from the mainland living in a remote nudist colony. He takes me back to his place, treats my foot with some type of fruit, and reduces the infection just enough for me to hike out of the backcountry and get to the hospital."

"*No way!*" I wanted to interject at least two curse words to emphasize my bewilderment but remained composed in their company.

"Ah, it was a long time ago. The kids were so little then. Good kids though—goofy and rambunctious. Kind. They were always kind. That, I believe, is the greatest praise I've ever received: being told my kids were kind"— his eyes glazed over in a long pause, his mind elsewhere— "I miss him. It's been so hard . . . well . . . you know . . . you understand."

"No. He *can't* understand," Julie interjected. "I'm sorry, but he just can't. No one can unless they've gone through it." It was almost paradoxical—this isolation of losing a child—with the way she didn't want anyone else to experience the pain she endured daily, but also wanted others with whom she could empathize and relate. The Boston Marathon bombing had happened only weeks earlier. And she wept. She wept because she understood the hardships these families now faced.

Hours passed as we delved further in stories. Of Nate. And he distracted: the plaque on the wall, the books dedicated in his honor, his countenance on Bob and Julie's faces. The best was my drink coaster: a photo of eight-year-old Nate stretching his mouth, with both hands, as far as possible. Goofy-ass Nate, as I picked up and put down my reverse-osmosis water. I was feeling things again. Mostly hurt.

My visit wasn't easy on them, either. I reminded them

of their son—our only tie, their only reason for knowing me. They asked about everything. They wanted to hear the perspective of his ghost from my mouth. And I couldn't convey just how powerful Nate's influence had been—not only to me, but to the thousands of people we met during our travels.

"I miss the way he used to keep the family connected," Julie said, "the way he would call everyone, always leaving voice messages, always saying: *I love you*. I especially miss how he would laugh at my jokes. No one else laughs at my stupid jokes!" She laughed, but not in the happy way.

As much as I was enjoying my visit, I knew my time with the Henns had come to an end. It'd become too much. Bob could hardly stay in the room, taking breaks to go outside, to process the rattled memories now falling from his mind like leaves in a storm.

I asked one final question: "Does it get any easier?"

"No," Julie answered, sharp and simple. "It's different now, but not easier. The first nine months were debilitating, like wearing ten x-ray vests they put on you at the dentist. It's an uncomfortable weight to bear. And it becomes your identity: I am a mother who has lost her son. It's the first thing you think about when you wake up and the last thing before going to bed. *I am a mother who has lost her son*."

Subtle pain hid in the Henns' words that day, unlike anything I'd ever heard. Maybe it was the fact that their son was taken in one quick explosion of utter inhumanity. Maybe it was the way they still held love and forgiveness in their hearts, the way they still relied on each other for support—marriage as intended.

I wanted to hold on to that moment, to Nate. They felt the same. Bob said goodbye, yet walked me to my rental car, lingering and awkward. He watched from a distance, forcing back tears and pacing, looking like a father sending his kid off to college. Supportive yet reluctant. He didn't want to see me go, a fleeting vestige of the son he wanted back.

Pulling out of the driveway and saying goodbye to Nate yet again, it happened. I broke open.

I hadn't felt much emotion in the years since Nate's passing. And despite showing little emotion in the Henns' house, I cried for the two hours back to my own parents. I contemplated my long-standing depression and my recurring suicidal thoughts, something I'd always known to be selfish and irrational, but never this dangerously transformative. My death—however it came—would change my family's identity, relationship, and unity. I couldn't bear to think about the long list of idiosyncrasies my own mother would miss about me; I couldn't bear to think about her reciting them to strangers. My dad would be shattered, too, shaken and irreparable—he would become that forever lingering image of Bob at the funeral.

Tears kept on, each sapping the pain and anger I'd been harboring somewhere deep inside my muted emotions, each deconstructing my internal Babel rising like a nightmare over every grave I've lain flowers upon. My fingers clenched the wheel. The Henns deserved better. They deserved relief. But there was nothing anyone could say or do to help. Because, as Julie made clear, it can't be understood. It can't. And yet, in some strange way, I now know that by living I can help protect others from ever having to understand it.

On my final day in North Carolina I said goodbye to my parents. Told them I loved them. The same repeated words now with new meaning. I returned to San Diego with clear eyes and a clean heart. I came back to find the dishes reaching for the heavens, to that same empty roll of toilet paper. I came back to a restored appreciation for the people who'd left it that way, my friends.

+

Halloween, and Other Acts of God
New York City, New York

———————

I was hell-bent on a good Halloween. Hell-bent on shocking my system and betraying any comfort zone that was keeping me from going out and getting wild. Because once you reach a certain age, once candy is no longer the core goal of the ghostly gala, Halloween becomes a gauge as to how lame you actually are—and if my past celebrations were any indication of still holding a strong social-life or tolerance for late nights, I was failing miserably. I was, by all intents and purposes, fucking lame.

But a good Halloween, that would prove I hadn't forsaken the promise of youth I still clutched, white knuckled, in a wilting grip; would prove I could put off being an adult for another season while still making those senseless mistakes more readily forgivable during adolescence. I'm talking a Halloween that exists only in the fragments of an alcohol-damaged mind, the kind starting with makeup and masks, claws and cloaks, but segues into darkness and drinking, psychedelics and sex. It would be a means of catching up.

I yearned for one of those random, freak-a-deak hook-ups with a gussied-up girl in promiscuous apparel—you know, that type of hook-up that doesn't mean anything romantically but leaves you feeling that special kind of hollow once mascara begins to smear; the type of hook-up where you might not learn the person's name, or even see their face, but is rewarded with weeks of worrying over an unwanted pregnancy, asymptomatic disease—or burning piss, maybe—because, of course, the whole affair was unprotected, quick, and would-be embarrassing if any level of sobriety had been involved. I was ready to pound ecstasy, cocaine, *whatever*, for this. Ready to give up pieces of myself that I could never get back—all for a destructive dream.

I wanted this because October 31 always found me accompanying my little brother, fifteen years my junior, around the neighborhood during his first several outings, or supervising my niece and nephews from door to door to door. Before that, during an age more expectant of partying—high school and university—I was a teetotaler with a long-term girlfriend. Or, as you may have known me, the judgmental asshole in the corner silently resenting everyone for being assholes, all the while jealous. And before that, at the age of vandalism and sabotage, I was too afraid of authority to ever smash a pumpkin or toilet paper a house.

That's why Halloween 2012—set to take place in New York City—had to be important. It flickered, like a jacko'-lantern flame, as my chance to right all the wrongs I'd committed. My chance to apologize for being so boring for so long and for never knowing what to do about it. I needed a good Halloween—if only for the story, for the peace of mind it would offer. And this was to be my year, everything coming together: the perfect city, the perfect costume, the perfect party. Nothing could stop me.

I bought the plane ticket five weeks before the holiday—San Diego to New York City and back again. This gave me and my friend Matt Woods, a Harlem resident, a month to plan the ideal night.

Matt's an artist who makes papier mâché taxidermied animals, howls at every full moon, and celebrates the dark, twisted gift that is life. I first met him in 2009 while working for Invisible Children: I stayed at his house for a week while touring the U.S., including Easter Sunday. I felt less homesick around him due to a tenderness in his countenance that juxtaposed with a commanding punk charisma: combat boots, tank tops over a skinny frame, a Mohawk bringing him closer to abolished gods. Little did I know then that he'd become one of my most reliant pen pals, the illustrator of my short stories, and my supreme educator on all things horror-film related.

Our plans already had a sturdy skeletal framework on which to apply flesh: an off-Broadway theater production called Sleep No More was throwing a carnival-themed party, and, from what I'd heard about this company's previous escapades, things were to get a pagan-kind of weird. (Supposedly, for their May Day festival, naked individuals circled the traditional pole of fertility, ribbons in hands, fake blood raining from the ceiling.) For our party, Matt and I were to be lions, accompanied, of course, by a friend dressed as the tamer.

The plan was brilliant—fucking brilliant—and I wasn't leaving New York City without my story. This was going to be the tall tale I could call upon whenever asked about Halloween. Forever free of the fear of remaining lame—

Then the unthinkable happened. A wrench in the fool-proof plan. A kink disrupting any hope of the kinky. And *she* was a real monster.

I first heard of her three days before my flight. When I bought the ticket I had no idea she'd been invited to the party—which, I suppose, she wasn't. She crashed it.

Big, black, and unforgiving. She came from the Caribbean, and I drew toward her, if only for the red flags raised in her approach, in every promise of destruction that gyrated from her very center of gravity. I wanted to dance with her—*dirty*—because she proved herself a stunner. A man-killer. A future horrid sob story.

Local reporters and national syndications were referring to her as the perfect storm. Others, of the more playful variety, called her "Frankenstorm." Her actual name was Sandy, chosen by the World Meteorological Organization, as with all other hurricanes that had come before her.

My flight made it to NYC just before the Eastern Seaboard started shutting down: airports, bus systems, subways. People were taking this shit seriously, and for good reason: the mayor of New York City, I'd been told, had underestimated the city's last natural disaster, a snowstorm, and was now overdoing the safety precautions. The city didn't need another embarrassing fiasco. But, by the end of the first day, nothing had happened. No Sandy, no downpour, just thunderheads on the horizon.

I holed up in Harlem, on an elevated section of the Manhattan Island, with Matt and a small collection of his cohort—neighbors, roommates, significant others. I looked to each girl as a potential accomplice to my master plan, so I threw out flirts to test the water, arguing the merits of *Friday Night Lights*, but got little engagement in return—my Westcoast sensibilities didn't mesh well with their more calloused East. Instead, I curled up with a Ray Bradbury book, *The Halloween Tree*, falling asleep alone.

The next morning, we awoke as kids on Christmas, eager to see what this "perfect storm" had delivered. The sky still looked nothing but overcast, destruction and devastation still just a rumor rustling in the leaves: no presents, no stockings. The day remained lazy, in atmosphere and attitudes, but something brewed, a witch's cauldron of clouds, an anticipation of hell being unleashed from the heavens above. We weren't quite feeling the threat yet, but prepared just the same, loading up on non-perishable goods, filling the bathtub with water, and accruing materials necessary to finish our *Lion King*-like costumes.

Then she came.

She came like a Greek god controlling the sea. Vengeful. With subways filling. Homes submerging. Infrastructure toppling and adding fire to the watery chaos, delivered by the wind from building to building to building. Thousands of houses were destroyed, a quarter of a million vehicles ruined, and dozens of lives lost. The total financial damage in the United States came to over $70 *billion*, an estimated 18 billion in New York City alone. Sandy became the second costliest hurricane in U.S. history, surpassed only by Katrina.

But for us, up in Harlem, the event felt somehow lackluster—a typical night of hanging out as rain pounded the apartment complex, the wind howling. Nothing escalated beyond that of a standard storm, and, I'm embarrassed to say, I went to bed disappointed.

It had been a dream to endure a natural disaster. The misadventure enchanting. Romantic. Like a quirky Disney movie, or a first date. Nervous energy. I feel it every time I enter a flash flood area or when I travel during cyclone season. It is beauty and mysticism, nature's unpredictable moods. And to be one of the few who get to experience its magnitude, to me, feels like a gift. A curse. A tragedy. A miracle.

This, of course, is easy to say when you're only a visitor to a city in distress. When it's not your home being destroyed. Not your neighbors' children drowning. But I was disappointed, suffice it to say. Sandy so close, yet unseen. She left me untouched, unafraid, unchanged. I awoke to the world just the same. Or so I thought. Then I went outside—

Debris laid everywhere. Fences knocked over. Trees unearthed. Cars crushed. Reports spoke of buildings missing entire front façades, their contents open to the world like giant doll houses. Of massive construction cranes toppling over. Of lower Manhattan losing all power. But the residents looked the most broken.

Matt and I later analyzed images on the Internet in disbelief: How could such a disaster have occurred, unnoticed, only miles away? And why didn't we try to get closer? Why didn't we meet her head on? The hurricane had come and gone, and we'd somehow failed to catch her in the act.

Despite it all, and my relative safety, Sandy did take something from me. Matt and I had busted our asses to finish our Halloween costumes, the result magnificent: handcrafted leather masks, shaped and molded with water-diluted Elmer's glue, hardened with a hair drier, then hand-painted and adorned with long strands of raffia.

Broadway-quality shit. But because of the destruction and loss of power in Lower Manhattan, the Sleep No More party had to be rescheduled for another day—a date long after my departure.

I sat in disbelief, petty in my sulking. Pathetic. Halloween became a low-key hangout. It became Chinese takeout and sobriety, an early night to bed. Sandy had torn through the city, taking lives and leaving thousands in dire circumstances, taking so much more than my silly dream. She had made Halloween a true nightmare.

Matt had to work the next day, All Saint's Day, so he drew me a map of Manhattan, marking each point of paramount destruction, and sent me on my way. I took the subway as far as it would allow, to 34th Street—anything below this point deemed dangerous: no power, nothing open, sea levels still high. So I walked into the belly of the beast.

What ensued resembled the apocalyptic. The eschaton. End of days. Lower Manhattan sat vacant, the streets void of cars, the sidewalks void of people. It was as if the city had been raptured and I got to play lone survivor to a world dressed as a movie set—nearly everyone missing from one of the busiest cities in the world.

I marched down 6th Street—down the middle of the road—walking lane markings like a tightrope, engulfed by buildings devoid of the life-blood of electricity. No horns resounded. No traffic formed. Manhattan belonged to me.

When I had to pee I went into Whole Foods, strangely open yet barren of all perishable goods. Customers looked lost, not really there to shop, lumbering and defeated. Ghosts to a new ghost town. When I needed to eat I lamented not having money. Being south of the electricity line, thrown back in to a dark age, I was traversing an all-cash economy—no one could take cards and no ATM was operational. Food trucks capitalized on the situation, making bank off the disoriented balance of supply and demand, casting the smell of sweet ambrosia into the air: foot-long polish dogs, falafel, fish tacos, gyros, cheesesteaks. The pang intensified. I kept on.

I passed humming generators and people wading through basements, both working to pump out the uninvited ocean. Others sat around in folding chairs, exchanging stories, listening to radios—a return to simpler times. The further I got from power, moving down the island, the bleaker things became. People lined for blocks near Union Square, eager for trucked-in dry ice to preserve any food left in their fridge. Over two million residents without power. My adventure was their horror, and I started to feel the weight.

I walked all the way to Battery Park, observed the statue that represents my liberty, and stared into dark clouds still lingering from the destruction. Rats scurried past, also displaced from their homes, with health officials saying rodents could start infesting areas in the city previously uninhabited by them, spreading the likelihood of typhus, salmonella, and hantavirus. I thought of my aunt Janice, seven years prior, contracting hantavirus while cleaning a pet store and then passing away unexpectedly, the disease so rare and identified too late, its early symptoms resembling the flu. Such death is never easy on a family—with lasting confusion, frustration, heartache—and Sandy was imparting it: over two hundred people from at least eight different countries died in that storm, the largest Atlantic hurricane on record, spanning 1,100 miles in diameter. An area larger than the size of Europe. I stared at its vestige—

Abject loss, rampant curiosity, basic needs unmet. My

mind slipped, losing touch, and I'd only been wandering for an afternoon. Imagine days. Weeks. I suppose that's when and why people begin to loot and pillage, overturning carts and taking what's needed, violent and raw, guns blazing and all that martial-law bedlam. I mean, you see it with every societal breakdown—*Lord of the Flies* scenarios of scalping and raping, intimidation and power struggles. Rwanda, Cambodia, the DRC. I look to the faces of revolutionary guerrillas, Islamic terrorists, rebel armies. I look inward.

I contemplated the uninhibited self and became fearful of my own species, knowing what chaos can pull from us. Things get ugly when resolve gets shaken, when comforts get stolen. And I knew I couldn't withstand the weight of my own moral codes tested against these natural or unnatural disasters. It was time to head back across that electricity line. My imagination needed boundaries and restrictions—the very reason I always sucked at Halloween. I need order. Structure. Procedure. I'd seen what I needed to see.

I spent nearly eight hours wandering in Sandy's wake, observing a city I will never experience in that way again. I felt the hurricane's salty kiss goodbye that day, an embrace I'd been longing for, but achieved in an unexpected way—something forever more fulfilling than that claimed from a stranger's lips.

I earned that once-in-a-lifetime story of which I longed. And now here I am, prideful and self-important, fully fed and bladder-emptied, to tell you that there is beauty in the breakdown. That there is even more beauty in the rebuilding. Because another flood occurred the day I left: that of the thousands of volunteers coming to help restore the city. The Red Cross alone raised more than

$200 million in donations by mid-December, mobilizing nearly sixteen thousand trained workers for response, almost all volunteers. Food and shelter became attainable. Reconstruction and rehabilitation proof of humanity.

We are a selfish species—selfishly surviving—but we are *good*. And we are learning. I had the perfect Halloween that year—the perfect one-night stand with Sandy—but I also witnessed the unexpected cost of it. I'm grateful to have my home and family intact. To be safe. I now appreciate trick-or-treating with my older brother's kids. And I'm content going to bed alone after an uneventful holiday. I'm grateful and content because I've witnessed the disasters this planet offers: in every fallen leaf, fallen façade, fallen friend. Because sometimes it takes an eclipse—something blocking our taken-for-granted light—to learn what we stand to lose. And the doom and gloom of those darker days still shine upon me.

+

The Final Fire
Black Rock City, Nevada

———————————

Dust grated the whites of my eyes as I wandered that desert, tears welling. I knew the moral of the story: never steal your best friend's romantic interest, especially when that friend is destined to die before you can apologize. Because guilt makes great tinder. That was the moral. Yet such enlightenment does little good when achieved after the fact. The desert seemed a good place to struggle.

For seven days I roamed, Wolf and I having joined a caravan containing gadgets and trinkets, masks and madness—my car filled to the brim. We traveled with a precise nowhere in mind, a wasteland that had made a name for itself. We followed the stars at night, sirens of the cosmic sea luring us deeper into darkness and back to the earth, back to the breath of God. That desert, unlike all others, was to be called Home. But that desert developed no differently—a range of mountains keeping it from rain. Maybe it's this destitution that inspires contemplation, but those mountains forced us to confront the catastrophes that forged the summits and sapped the soil dry.

We'd climbed many mountains together, Wolf and I, but now found ourselves in a vast, lonely expanse filled with fifty-thousand other people. Burning Man.

My fascination with Burning Man didn't start with ecstasy-driven dreams of dancing through the night, free-love fantasies of sexual exploration, or utopian ideologies of perpetuating an experimental apocalypse. For me, it was about religion.

My religion started with a much-too-early curiosity about divinity, exhausting thoughts on good and evil when I should've been pursuing a first kiss and playing peewee football with friends. I began reading the Bible, the Koran, the Mahabharata, various sutras, and the Tao Te Ching when I should've been reading *The Catcher in the Rye*, *To Kill a Mockingbird*, or *The Great Gatsby*. I had questions left unanswered, doubts unchecked, and a waning belief in any existential purpose. I began resenting the faithful around me, becoming another angry atheist. Yet I yearned for the belief—any belief—others around me held. With time, this resentment turned to understanding, once I realized that religion is more than the institutions it's pigeonholed as. Though faithless, religion held my fascination.

That's how I became a religious studies graduate student at the University of South Florida in the spring of 2009—my focus on religion within popular culture. The subject was relatively new to academia and addressed how the two subjects interrelate: when myth and ritual are used in concert, almost anything can be considered religion. Things like the sacrament of sports, Disneyland, diet fads, and *Star Trek* fandom. It includes Burning Man.

I first read about the annual festival from a scholarly viewpoint, in an article analyzing the event's powerful use of ritual, myth, and symbolism. Once aware of Burning Man, it started popping up everywhere: students discussing it; professors sharing stories of attending; photos circulating the Web.

Burning Man had humble beginnings on the shore of Baker Beach in San Francisco in the early 1980s. Friends would meet to participate in a bonfire ritual during the summer solstice, including the construction and subsequent burning of a clumsy effigy at the event's culmination. These effigies became increasingly more elaborate: over three years' time the structure grew from eight feet, to fifteen feet, to forty feet. It started being referred to as "the Man."

Permits and city liability eventually became an issue, so the event joined with another group holding their own radical sculpture burnings and theatrics out in the Black Rock Desert of northern Nevada. The combination, plus word-of-mouth, sprouted the beginnings of Black Rock City—the origin of Burning Man as it's known today.

The celebration fuses artwork to community to absurdity, and it operates on basic principles, including self-reliance, self-expression, leave-no-trace, gifting, and decommodification—all basically meaning the desert is dangerous and unforgiving, that people will be doing weird shit with their bodies (and other people's, too), that a cash economy is not allowed, and that commercialism can go fuck itself. Burning Man is every suppressed

mania—induced by the backwards logic of Western culture—set free. It's your wildest wet dream on hard, hard
drugs. Burning Man is the day of creation wrapped in a
dirty film of dust and self-discovery.

But Burning Man is also religion—a religion that ag-
nostics like me can study via participation. A dormant
seed was planted and Burning Man came to hold a nag-
ging spot in the back of my thoughts. It needed a trigger
for growth.

My muse came as Matt Woods one year later. When
Matt first mentioned his interest in attending Burning
Man, and said he'd made a pact to go before his twenty-
seventh birthday, I agreed to the challenge. Matt was born
three days before me, and in 2011 we both turned twenty-
seven. His pact became mine.

Not much later I received a text from Mr. Woods:
Tickets go on sale today . . . should we do it? The question was
rhetorical: by the end of the day (after spending countless
hours on an Internet queue and hundreds of dollars), we
had tickets. In eight months we'd be traveling 110 miles
north of Reno to become citizens of Black Rock City and,
unbeknownst to us joining the largest gathering of Burning Man participants to date—fifty-thousand strong.

Black Rock City, for one week, would become the
sixth largest city in Nevada. The theme that year was "Rite
of Passage" and Burning Man's twenty-fifth anniversary.
By happenstance we'd selected an important time to attend.

In August, Matt flew to Montana to meet me. From
there we hit the road, replica Lost Boys destined for the
desert: slacks cut into pirate pants, unlaced boots, bandan-
as sewn together as decorative tails, formal vests covering
our bare upper bodies, utility belts securing homemade

slingshots and wooden swords. We transformed under ca-
nine hoods: Fox and Wolf. We were men acting as kids
and kids acting as animals in the harsh terrain—dust, heat,
wind. Your classic case of man versus nature. But, unbeknownst to Matt at the time, there was another conflict at
hand: man versus self.

One year prior, Nate died in Uganda. The reality still
haunted. A life I'd loved had not only been lost, but stolen
through cold murder. Terrorism is a weird thing to process
when it becomes more than George W.'s child-like play at
war. When someone you know is the target of terrorism
you start to fancy yourself an authority on the matter, as
if you, more than anyone else, have the right to speak on
it. To curse it. To hate it.

With time, though, anger begins to subside. Wounds
convert to scars. But as my deepest lesion hardened back
to health, something else festered. Shame.

I still hadn't forgiven myself for pursuing the girl that
Nate had liked.

Matt and I first stopped at Yellowstone National Park and
then Craters of the Moon National Monument, climbing
through lava tubes and hiking mountains of volcanic ash.
Tails blew wild in the wind. When we finally made it to
our Reno hotel room, our last night in civilization, we met
up with the cohort we'd be camping with: Kostume Kult.

Kostume Kult is a New York-based group of Burning
Man regulars who supply costumes at the event: the prem-
ise of Burning Man being that you provide some sort of
service to the community. The barter/gift-giving system
at work. Everyone does their part. Kostume Kult is continually in good favor with the Burning Man city planners

and therefore gets a prime camping spot on the Esplanade, the inner-most road of the semi-circular city. The Esplanade has the most magnificent view of all the artwork—especially the Man. Kostume Kult sets up a dome on the Esplanade and fills it with three tons of costumes accumulated throughout the year. They dress anyone who comes into the tent, the only price is that you walk the fashion runway.

Matt's friend Amanda hooked us up with Kostume Kult. She's the one Matt originally made the age pact with, and in Reno we added Amanda and her friend Jennifer to our immediate team.

"I hear the dust has so much—what's it called, Jen?"

"Alkaline."

"Yeah! Alkaline! I hear it has so much alkaline that if you go barefoot your skin will *literally* start to blister." Amanda sat on the hotel room floor folding clothes. Jen stood across the room wearing nothing but panties, an elaborate and beautiful weave of colorful dread-like strands draping down her exposed skin. I couldn't remember the last time I'd seen a naked woman, and yet this occasion seemed so nonchalant. So nonsexual.

"I hope the dust doesn't ruin my hair, at least for the first few days. It took so long to put this shit in," Jen said, digging through her suitcase, repacking for efficiency. "Oh, look what I brought us." She dumped a bag of electronic necklaces and flashing jewelry on the bed, making a slight squeal. "Take whatever you want. You gotta be visible at night so you don't get run over!"

"You serious about the alkaline?" I asked.

"Wear boots, you'll be fine," Amanda answered, putting on a string of illuminated skulls. "Or soak your feet in vinegar at night. It somehow counteracts the chemicals."

"My biggest question"—Matt chimed in, looking at the luggage—"is how the *fuck* are we going to fit all this in the car?"

The next morning a Tower of Babel rose from the roof of my Santa Fe as we piled and bungeed suitcases, tents, and bicycles skyward. Junk brimmed so that I couldn't see the girls sitting in the back, and they couldn't see each other. We rode like this for the three hours to Black Rock City, then for the six hours of waiting to get in.

Our slow-rolling tires crushed dormant landscape, breaking the crust into fine powder that caught in the wind, a veil of white haze blending into the sky and fading into the distance: airborne alkaline for our eyes, our lips, our lungs. *Be prepared for the dust*, everyone advised before coming. Now, I understood. Black Rock was unlike any place I'd seen—nothing grew there. No weeds. No scrub. This holy ground and holy ghost, it's what they called the playa. People said you could see the curve of the earth, the horizon endless and uninterrupted, a sea of beige from bypassed rainfall.

Burners got out of their cars as they waited, chatting with strangers and offering entertainment. Girls hula hooped on RVs ahead of us. Nude bodies weaved in and out of sight. One vagabond knocked on my window—a woman offering blueberries she'd just spilled across the ground. "Dust gets everywhere anyway," she shrugged, eating one. I followed suit. It tasted of talc: gritty, earthy, and yet somehow soft. Mixing with my mouth's moisture, it turned to cake, sticking to my teeth and inner lips, a taste I'd come to know well.

At the entrance gate—a scene of vigilante law—inspection occurred: staff poked around our luggage, glanced at our tickets, asked basic questions. Everything fine. Yet they didn't know what I hid in my heart. Neither did I. But as the blueberry almsgiver had suggested, dust was to leave nothing untouched.

Almost permitted to enter Black Rock City, we faced one final question: "Ever been to the Burn before?" We shook our heads. "All right, get out of the car." We had to ring a giant bell, roll in the dust, and yell, "I'm not a virgin anymore!" We had arrived.

Pulling in to our site, a man identified as Jungle (looking like Mel Brooks) approached the car in nothing but a toga, knocking with urgency. "Welcome Home," he said. Home: what everyone calls the playa.

"Jungle?" I asked Matt.

"He decorates his RV like a jungle . . . it's a playa name. They get assigned to you by other people. It's easy to meet someone out here and never actually learn their name. Like that guy—that's Noodle because he fucked up cooking the noodles during his first burn. I have no idea what his real name is."

I met Rocket, Costume Jim, and Boris the Elf. Night encroached as we set up camp and met others from Kostume Kult, nearly two-hundred. I started to gain my bearings as I found Center Camp (a place with coffee and ice), the closest row of porta potties, and the Esplanade. The city seemed endless—unfathomable in the short time I had with it—the municipal design as if a giant "C" had been imprinted on the earth with the middle open for art installments. At the very center stood the Man: a crude geometric figure, like a child would draw, standing atop two triangular pinnacles with a chasm between them, the Man with one foot on each and reaching a height of ninety feet.

With waning natural light, the desert illuminated in

artificial neon: on participants, on bicycles, on mutant cars—the only motorized vehicles allowed to cruise the playa, having been crafted into dragons, pirate ships, and narwhals. Spotlights of various hue shot to the heavens and circled the perimeter. Fire exploded from metallic contraptions. A landscape transformed. Other worldly. A cosmic dance of mischief. As if Vegas had hosted a rave sponsored by Satan himself.

Despite the theatrics, I went to bed early, recouping from the drive. I had six more nights to be festive.

The next morning spawned Tutu Tuesday: Kostume Kult announced themes daily. I dressed in boots, old professional wrestling trunks, a black and pink tutu, and, of course, the fox hat. Not long after I met Steph. "Anyone wanna go for a *run?*" she asked, looking to us lounging around camp under the hangar-like shade structure.

"A run? Are you kidding me?" I asked, the temperature easily over a hundred degrees.

"No, a *ride*, dummy. A bike ride." This girl had Mediterranean features coupled with an Australian accent, gorgeous and quirky. Patron saint of patron saints, Steph.

We rode into the expanse of art, both in tutus. "Tell me something interesting about yourself," I said.

"How about a prompt?"

"Teeth."

"I'm embarrassed to say this, but I sucked my thumb far beyond the point of being cute. Into grade school." She smiled something enchanting and bashful—perfect teeth, perfect charm . . . I didn't stand a chance. "Now *you* tell me something embarrassing!"

"I used to collect *Star Wars* action figures. Hundreds of them, all still in their packages. I could probably recite the name of each toy for you, too. I was obsessed. Never

helped with dating though, as I'm sure you can imagine."
She laughed in agreement.

"I wanna get pancakes," she said. "And then we can
visit the Temple." The Temple: the only Burning Man
structure rivaling the grandeur of the Man. And though
the Man represents the collective of the Burn, the Temple
holds its spirit—the holiest of holies. Each year the Temple varies in design and resides in the gap where the C-
shaped city opens. That year "the Temple of Transition"
had a main, 120-foot hexagonal central tower. Five smaller
towers surrounded of the same design, each reminiscent
of Japanese pagodas. Everything connected to the center
by ascending bridges, and was cut with gothic-style arches
of whites and subtle yellows. Living art. Evolving art. The
most powerful part of the structure was graffiti, decipher-
able only upon close inspection.

Inside the Temple with Steph, I began noticing: messages in Sharpie covered every inch. Participants had come
to turn their inner torment into text. A message in black:
*I love and miss you so much . . . I owe you so much . . . all of my
heart.* In red: *I have only three weeks to live & I decided to spend
one at Burning Man.* In Green: *Suicide sucks! Ben I will miss you
forever.* Pictures hung nearby.

It was a temple, but also a monument to loss, longing,
and forgiveness. It mesmerized. It stirred. My favorite part
of the city. But my attention, at that moment, remained
with Steph, mesmerizing and stirring in her own right. We
talked from the elevated platform overlooking the playa,
time ceasing to exist.

Then she took me to Costco.

Its full title was Costco Soulmate Trading Outlet, a
camp and service that helped participants find their Burning Man soul mate. This included first a questionnaire and

then an interview. You could return the next day and receive the name and location of the person who they felt best suited you. They would, in turn, give your name and location to someone else, a different person than you were given.

We sat crammed on a couch, the place packed, filling out surveys under the midday heat. Dozens of questions, the last one stinging: *Do you have any regrets?* I had one in mind.

When they called my name, I met my interviewer, a badge reading "Sarah." She wore a Costco apron—that was all she wore. Glancing around, she noticed the state of affairs, and concluded there was only room to sit in the dirt, cross-legged. Her humble breasts could not be concealed by the narrow apron. And yet, as in the hotel with Jen, there was nothing intimate about the interaction—she meant business.

This is what I loved about Burning Man, and one of the best lessons I learned: the body, like the place I'd just visited, was a temple. But what pop culture had built in my brain remained radically different from the temples nature intended. Augmentation and diet fads, fast food and corn syrup reshaped our structures, curved our contours, altered our anatomy. Hollywood, porn, and my peers had taught me to praise something different. My "naked" was artificial, immaculate, a false idol. Now, before me, sat the iconoclast—proof of the actual.

During the Burn I would see bodies with sag, fat, pale in color, failing in posture, speckled with moles. These were bodies I'd been taught to judge unattractive; and yet these were *actual* human bodies. In that moment, with Sarah, I realized how few "real" naked bodies I'd seen—and I, the clothed one, felt ashamed.

There she sat, the type of girl who'd probably never worked a day at the actual Costco, who'd boycott shopping at the big-box store altogether. Regardless, we went over my two-page application, and I did my best to stay focused on her eyes. When we got to the final question she said, "All it says is *I kissed the wrong girl.* What's that even mean?"

I told her the story—shrapnel, punctured lungs, regret-flavored fooling around. I told her. And she wept. Yet I sat emotionless, broken to that method of healing. "I'm a counselor in the default world," she continued, wiping tears. "You should go see someone about this. I run a support group here on the playa—you could come if you wanted. I want you to come, please?"

"I'm just kinda here to find a soul mate," I mumbled, diverting my eyes. To this she gave me a hug—her bare chest against mine, her tear-streaked face so foreign. I was this desert, this dust.

The next day was the Horned Ball, meaning everyone from Kostume Kult had some sort of antler, spike, or prong attached to their head. Amanda, a makeup artist, mounted two demonic and bone-like horns to my temples. Cosmetics of blood and torn flesh made the emergence appear painful.

Matt (now Wolf to my eyes) and I (now Fox to his eyes) walked to Center Camp for coffee. A monster approached in transit, about six feet tall, its body white and furry, hands and feet massive and black, face elongated and made of Velcro. It frowned.

"Help Monster, please," it said.

"Okay, what do you need?" Wolf asked.

"New face," it said, handing Wolf a purse containing various facial expressions. "Monster clumsy," the beast la-

mented. Wolf rearranged its face into something less somber, something less lonely.

"Don't worry," I told it, "I was monster-clumsy once,
too."

Back at our own camp, coffee in hand, I couldn't get
over the previous day: Steph, the Temple, the interview.
Trouble brewed, the harshness of the desert wearing on
my senses. I tried writing:

Fox and Wolf go to the Moon

*Wolf came to visit. He was looking for adventure. Fox obliged, so
they went to the moon. Fox led the way, as he had sailed the cosmos
before. Wolf asked no questions. He was more than ready to dance
in the craters' gloom.*

*They crawled, they climbed, they leapt, they roamed. They trans-
formed the landscape of the desolate, and the moon was alive with
dirt and dust as their tails blew wild in the wind.*

*Time passed as their once-vibrant coats began to mat—there
was no one to impress on the moon. They circled the earth, time and
again. They circled, hearts aching a little more with each orbit. For
Wolf, in all his glory, had come to find while on the moon he had no
moon to howl at. And Fox was troubled too, for on the moon he had
no moonlight to hide in. They had both forgotten the art of being
sly—their curious ears no longer sitting so high.*

*But wolves will be wolves, and foxes the same—they were lonely
and needed to go back home. However, this time they'd wandered too
far and were never to come back from such a great spin. So there
they remained, Fox and Wolf, alone and left to howl at the earth . . .*

Left to howl at the earth.

My literary outlet didn't help. I took a walk, drawn
back to the Temple. I ran fingers along plywood, watching people perform yoga under the central tower. Others

prayed. One guy cleansed my chakras using a prayer bowl. Many religions were represented—Hinduism, Buddhism, Christianity, Islam, Judaism, Taoism, Jainism—everything that had brought me there.

Grabbing a Sharpie, as my own prayer, I left a message. I wrote to my aunt who had died several years earlier from hantavirus, a rare pulmonary syndrome, airborne and contracted by inhaling rodent excreta. Death by nature's choosing.

Thursday meant pajamas and I squeezed into a onesie several sizes too small. Everything bulged. Wolf, Steph, and I consulted the Burning Man manual for things to do: Slut Touch Aerobics, Advanced Lucid Dreaming Kung Fu, and Irish Zombie Movie Night. We settled on a Ted Talk.

I ended up back on the streets, unaccompanied. My pattern didn't really match up to anyone else's because most people were consuming copious drugs, staying up all night, and going to bed at dawn—right when I was waking up. Also, I wasn't doing drugs—not because I disagreed with them, but because I had to avoid any stimulant that triggered my depression. So I wandered while others slept, alone in my thoughts. This desert of radical self-expression, of dust storms and mid-day heat waves, became the perfect place for such reflection—the flat, sun-bleached playa, my mirror to the heavens. And the Temple drew me back, its lure too strong. That afternoon I left another pen-to-plywood prayer. This one for Good Ol' Johnny Boy, having killed himself five months prior. I didn't blame him or condemn his decision, only felt sorry about the hand he was dealt. His death by contemplation.

That night my schedule coincided with Steph's and we walked the beat together, checking out favorite art installments. Everything transformed from day to night: the people, the art, the Man. I didn't feel so alone with her. She listened. And I wanted to be known.

I was fighting tooth and claw to fend off that sick disease called loneliness. But kissing, as I learned a year prior, isn't the cure. Another's touch could never compensate for the void that's left when they're gone. Being comfortable in your own skin—your temple—that's the lasting asylum.

Steph and I shared favorite songs through shared headphones as we walked back to camp, but surrendering to separate tents. She didn't want me the way I wanted her—another girl on my long list of "what if's."

That night I dreamt of a slaughterhouse I could do nothing to stop. Because something still haunted me. I still owed someone an apology.

Friday meant pirates. With my nails painted black and bead-braided hair, I wrote another message—to Shane. It'd been eight years since his passing, the toughest of the lot because it was the first lesson in critical loss: accidental death and it could have been any of us. But it was Shane, and now I couldn't remember his face, his laugh, his personality. He was now the *idea* of death, and being the good friend he was, he'd prepared me for my future.

I wrote feverishly, ink to wood as if it were the black blood in my veins. Each message was somehow setting me free—at least I'd hoped—but still, I felt shame, avoiding the real message I needed to write.

Back at camp a new sign hung over the entrance: *No Soul Mates Allowed.* The creepy reappearance of Costco participants had become a problem. This was the day things began to burn, specifically the minor art—fire claiming years' worth of investment, creation, and dedication. I watched my favorite piece, a circular dragon swallowing its own tail, go up in flames. The coup de grâce of the evening was a replica Trojan horse, sixty-feet tall, assaulted with flaming arrows. Kostume Kult mock-raided other camps this night in honor of the pirate theme. But as a Lost Boy at heart, and despising all pirates, I opted to go to bed early yet again. Wolf lost his sword that night but stole a compass, regaining direction and returning home with the rising sun.

By Saturday all the art had been destroyed, everything except the Man and the Temple. I went for a walk, alone and not looking for much. Steph had started hanging out with another guy, avoiding my company. Wolf was off with other friends. And I was feeling dejected even though it was me keeping people at arm's length and then condemning them for not accepting, loving, and revering me enough. But I'd been living in fear of another death, whether literal, emotional, or metaphorical. Afraid of that sweet depression that made me want to die.

Because I don't want another phone call bringing bad news. I can't carry another casket. Can't do another late-night visit to the cemetery, whether to stop a friend with a knife or to say "Hey" to a corpse already in the ground. To say, "I'd like to buy you a beer." To say, "I'd be nice to hear you laugh," or, "I don't trust people sticking around since you left." Worst of all, "I miss you."

I started to sob, feeling lost, tired, and defeated by the dust. Because the desert rends your heart, fighting to cleave the two halves apart, re-breaking every healed crack you thought you'd sealed, and then it feeds you the bounty—the prize—your own bitter heart. But my internal desertification was ending. I had to make a final trip to the Temple.

My last message percolated up, spontaneous words on

wood, not the script I'd written in my head every day since that bomb went off in Kampala. And though the message was addressed to Nate, it was meant for me.

Because Nate was gone, and although we'd never discussed it, he'd already forgiven me while he was still alive. I knew this. I just couldn't come to forgive myself. But everything, in that single moment, became simple and perfect. I wrote in the phantom company of fifty-thousand others who had come to purge and lock away their troubles, too.

That night the Man burned. First slowly, building heat, the wood refusing its fate. Participants were slow to ignite, too, staring confused—this was the moment that was supposed to define the event. This was "the Burn." But it was meek. Everyone anticipating. Waiting. Putting ecstasy and acid on their tongues. Waiting. Mutant cars parked and idling. The desert night cold and crisp. Then something caught, the flame growing skyward, exponentially, a blazing pillar at least 100 feet in height. Fireworks erupted. And everyone turned savage, the night becoming a blur of neon with participants screaming as if on a warpath, sprinting circles around the flame. Cars blared horns. Desert hippies groped and open-mouth kissed. Complete frenzy. And I lost my cohort to the shuffle, standing alone in the madness. It was the same primeval lunacy I'd felt on Red Mountain, the necessary havoc required for order to come out of chaos. For peace to restore in one's heart. To break open—and regrow.

Sunday morning, people started leaving. You could see the default world regretfully returning to their eyes. Deconstruction began, of camps and of minds. The Burn was nearly over and all that was left—alone and ominous over the playa, like a mountain over a desert—was the Temple of Transition. Those of us who were left shared an unspoken bond.

Burning Man is religion—religion which I'd studied by living it. But more than a study, it became an experience, and now I stood closer to the community and healing power and belonging I'd so desperately wanted all my life. Doubts and unanswered questions fell away. They no longer mattered.

We labored all day—cleaning up—and that night made our hajj to the Temple of Transition. Tens of thousands circled the structure, friends all around: Steph to my front, Wolf by my side. And the burning started. The final fire.

I grabbed Wolf by the hand and we howled from our hearts: at the earth we were returning to, at the clumsy monsters we had been, at everything we had burned to get there.

This was my Temple, flames consuming the past week, the past twelve months, the past twenty-seven years. We were hundreds of yards from the messages I had written—that we'd all written. They were turning to ash. And come tomorrow, none of this will have existed.

I wish I could recall what they said, all those messages scrawled from my misery and remembrance. I wish I could recount every word, and prove my heart, my lament, and my sincerity. I wish I could say what accepting death and truly saying goodbye feels like. What self-forgiveness *feels* like.

But I can't. That's not how letting go works. Yet, I still hear them—the mountains, the rivers, the deserts. *Have I made you happy yet?* they ask. And I nod. I exhale. I breathe.

I let go. My final fire. My restoration—out of the wilderness like a column of smoke. Finally, my friends, fianlly, I let go.

+

The Body

Epilogue

For nearly ten years I circled, migrating from one new hope to the next—professional wrestling, religious studies, Invisible Children, the chateau in Colorado, national parks—accruing many additional homes and making many difficult decisions along the way. Enduring hard farewells. But then I finally landed, a nesting ground—I found writing.

I moved *home*, to Montana, because I need the Mountain West. Because there is an allure here, under the Bridger Range, to keep you around, or at least to keep calling you back. It's the open space, both above and beyond. It's bison on the prairie, it's the pink of bitterroot against gravel, it's a red-winged blackbird on each fence post marking the way to your dying grandfather's house. It's knowing that

Montana has decent soil, though stubborn and rocky, to give a used-up body back to. It's where I come from, it's who I am, and you can't take it out of me—not without leaching the very marrow from my bones. Because like a flower to a seed, we don't get to decide how we grow, only how we reach for the sun. And literature was turning me toward the light.

I moved back with the intention of finishing a first book. I thought it was going to be fiction, maybe a novel or short stories, but I kept being pulled, cathartically, to non-fiction. To essays. To my lessons on loss. And I knew, to evolve into the writer I wanted to become, I had to serve my muse: death, it seemed, would be my subject matter. But before I could commence, there was one last thing I needed to do. One last trail I needed to hike . . .

Four years after the Kampala bombings, and after visiting forty-three of the fifty-nine U.S. national parks, I returned to Longs Peak. I'd set the goal of summiting Longs because of Nate's death. It made sense at the time: overcome a mountain and overcome loss. So I returned to finish what I'd started, because it was time to place the capstone on a half-decade of hurt. To give a four-year curse back to the heavens. To say: I will forever miss the way you smiled, I will always love you, and goodbye.

But as absurd as life can be, death wasn't done with me. There was one last lesson to learn.

While hiking the trail I happened upon a body, a near-naked figure, bloody and dashed against an adjacent rock face. I wasn't the first one to spot him. Nor the second. Nor the twentieth. Foot traffic was heavy that July morning, and, even with a 4 a.m. start, I was late to the trail.

Many others had come to the carnage before me. A human body.

I just stared.

I stared because perceptions change at such an altitude. Death is different in the wild. No one told me to keep moving or to look away; no one covered the body or tried moving the remains. The only acknowledgment of the scene came from a descending hiker: "Just to let you know, there's a body up there. It's gruesome."

Like everyone else, I had to walk through and step over the gore: blood, brains, and other organs. The deceased man had fallen from Longs Peak, the highest point in northern Colorado, becoming the sixtieth victim of the monolith in the past hundred years. Search and Rescue wouldn't get to the scene to remove the remains for a couple hours.

I knew there were dangers inherent in the hike, something I'd learned four years prior, but this was the starkest of reminders. I messaged friends, with the little service available, to tell them that if they heard the news, it wasn't me, I was safe.

They were already worried, especially my mom, and for good reason: summiting Longs requires dicey scrambling up and around the twisting peak, where wind becomes more than an annoyance and lightning a real threat. Thousands of optimistic hikers turn around each year, just short of the summit, realizing the last mile and a half isn't worth the risk.

I was one of those people, having failed Longs on my first attempt. In the time between then and now, I had dreamt about, cursed, and revered the mountain. I had seen it etched on state quarters, found it documented in articles, and heard it whispered by fellow travelers.

But moving up the peak this time, during my second attempt at the mountain, I had to ask myself was it actually worth it. Every four or five steps I had to stop to catch my breath—to rest my head on a boulder—and muster all sapped confidence to continue. Every fifty feet I debated turning around, I debated lying and telling everyone I had made it, and then never returning. But I kept on.

When I made the summit I felt no elation, only relief. One man congratulated me upon arrival, but I said nothing in response—due to lack of oxygen in my lungs and to a lingering sense of shame in my heart. I mean, what the fuck was I doing up there? I'd seen what death does to a family, to friends, and I was foolishly compromising my safety on such an irrelevant task. There was a body not far below to prove it—his family, somewhere, soon to be grieving. Friends mourning. The cycle renewed.

But the location of the fall had me surprised: it really wasn't that dangerous of a spot. The guy must have been trekking where he didn't belong, way off trail. And this made me consider all of the times my friends and I had ventured off trail, climbing things where our hands didn't belong and where our skills didn't suffice. I am guilty of the most irrational outdoor decisions, of believing in biological invincibility. But this body, now an empty vessel, soon to bloat and wither and liquefy, told a different cautionary tale. Something wasn't right . . .

I knew in my gut what it was—suicide.

When I later postulated this theory to friends they all said the same thing: *Anyone who respects the trail wouldn't do that to other hikers.* I thought maybe they were right. I hoped they were. But I just kept revisiting that scene in my mind—

On the way back down from the mountain, I'd spent

more time with the body. I could see everything but his head, hidden behind a boulder—the boulder that had stopped his fall. I was tired, nearly crawling, and placing my hands on the blood-splattered rocks just to keep my momentum going. It was grotesque, his DNA on my fingers, but I decided to sit with him longer. I stared longer.

I stared because we have resigned death to an illicit "holy other." We hide bodies quickly, we dress them in false presentation, we fabricate elaborate stories as to what comes next. We call it everything except for what it actually is: natural.

Maybe that's because death is no longer natural, not with the way we poison water tables, saturate foods with unnecessary additives, and drop bombs on our own brothers and sisters. Death becomes murder, car accidents, and cancer. Death becomes occupational: those who are meant to see it do; those who aren't don't. But I was seeing it. And it was beautiful.

It was beautiful because it was the raw and organic version of reality that our society, in recent years, has so desperately sought. No bullshit. No hidden ingredients. Only death. And to have those long moments with just him and me, and an undistorted truth, was beautiful.

Months later, after continually checking for an update, I read the coroner's report—and my heart sank. An eighteen-year-old kid. A suicide.

I don't know why I needed the confirmation. Maybe this death was the conclusion to my era of loss. Maybe it was permission to stop searching, to stop hurting, to move forward. But I weep for him, this kid, a person I will never meet, because that kid was me—not but ten years prior—had I taken that leap.

I needed him. As permission to forgive myself. To

forgive my depression. Because after those four long years—after a deep crevasse of time and torment had settled between the milestones of that same mountain peak—there I was staring down death yet again, no longer a stranger, nor a coward, to its presence. I'd made my peace. I'd reached that summit.

But still I weep for him, this kid on Longs Peak, hoping his torment is gone. Hoping, like me, that he found the peace and forgiveness he went wandering for.

Acknowledgements

———

Art, like an ecosystem, depends on collaboration. The assembled web is sheer, thin sinews keeping disparate parts connected to a whole. I cannot begin to acknowledge the holistic inner workings of this book because, as with ecology, the labyrinth of fibers remains unknown to me. Here is my attempted at giving praise where praise is due.

To my family, that is Bruce, Loretta, Treaver, Troy, Rebecca, Andrew, Landon, Max, and Natalie. You are my lifeblood, a sounding board for all my idiocy, and a reminder that love is enough to live. You save me daily.

To my early readers and editors: Dale McCarthy, Joe Tromsness, Seth Williams, Steph Karayannis, Shawn Hystad, Rebekka Esbjornson, and especially Dennis Held. Writing is embarrassing—you all endured the sentences, paragraphs, and entire essays that got cut.

To my literary and outdoor communities: the Beargrass Writing Retreat, the Bread Loaf Orion Environmental Writers' Conference, the Thunderhead Writers' Collective, the Bozeman Poetry Collective, Pecha Kucha Bozeman, Elle Brooks and Wake Up and Write (where I derived the title for this collection), the Country Bookshelf, REI Bozeman (that is, Teresa Larson), Active.com (that is, Michelle Valenti Hollenbeck), Cafe M of Belgrade, the Spotted Horse Cafe, the American Prairie Reserve, the Della Terra Mountain Chateau, the National Park Service, and any writing group (especially the Rick Bass crew who helped me with "Blood Ties") who have included me in their company.

To all dirt bags who have pursued art with me: Chad Houseman aka Tom Hymn, Matt "Wolf" Woods (for whom I have the grimmest of love), Raf Deza and The Avenue, Michelle Tobias, Heather Nation, Z.G. Tomaszewski, Alex Newby, my droogs (Brian Mulder, Jeffrey Niemeier, DJ Viernes, Pierangelo Grosso), Nigel McGuinness, Zach Barrows, Phillip Harder, Daniel J. Rice, Dana Perry, Taylor Brorby, Emily Freeman, Rachel Ashley, Haley Morris, Kelly Mullins, Carson Evans, Nada Alic, Andrew Koji Shiraki, the boys of Lee Corey Oswald, Allison Weiss, and Chris Farren. To my pen pals (letter writing is not dead). To anyone who has created zines with me, to anyone who has visited national parks with me, and to anyone who has hosted a house-show reading at my behest.

To Chad Clendinen (and Liz DeZeeuw for enduring all those late-night voiceover edits) for asking to make a film about my story—and for following through. The project is what persuaded me to release this book. Your friendship is an anchor. Also in relation to the film: Nathan Garcia, Jason and Danica Russell, Reece Long, Jason

Begin, Anna Schuck, Brit Chreptyk, Bethany "Wendybird" Bylsma, Hannah Jones, Angela Diange Bentley, the Telluride Mountainfilm Festival, and the HumaNature podcast. Steve Witmer, you were the first to believe in my writing and I am forever grateful—thanks, as always, for the beautiful design work. To our Kickstarter supporters, specifically Prasanna Sritharan and Siv Yoganathan, Shannon Constable, John Rudolph Beaton, JoLeah and Brian Gorman, Rob Lutz, Rob Wasel. To Invisible Children and everyone who agreed upon the fact that the use of child soldiers is unacceptable and not to be ignored.

To the people represented in these essays. To their families. To their friends. Specifically the Henn family (particularly Brynne, Kyle, Bob, and Julie), the Thomas family (Trev, you are a brother), Arnie Bowers, the Kelly family, the Kings and Gustafsons, Grandma Sis, Unc Donnie. To the families who've lost their loved ones on Longs Peak. Writing about death is a delicate terrain to tread—I meant no harm as far as my version of these truths could allow and I apologize for any wounds revisited.

Suicide sucks. Depression sucks. OCD sucks. Talk about your troubles. Get help. Build snowmen.

And please stay connected: join my monthly newsletter (tylerdunning.com/contact-1/) or find me on Instagram (@tylerdunning). Eat green things. Protect this wild world. Create art. Give it to someone. Keep sharing these roots. Keep growing.

About the Author

———

Tyler Dunning grew up in southwestern Montana, developing a feral curiosity and reflective personality at a young age. This mindset has led him around the world, to nearly all of the U.S. national parks, and to the darker recesses of his own creativity. He's dabbled in such occupations as professional wrestling, archaeology, social justice advocacy, and academia. At his core he is a writer.

Watch his accompanying short film, also titled "A Field Guide to Losing Your Friends," at tylerdunning.com.

Other Titles From Riverfeet Press

available at: riverfeetpress.com

THIS SIDE OF A WILDERNESS: A Novel (2013)
- Daniel J. Rice

THE UNPEOPLED SEASON: Journal from a North Country
Wilderness (2014)
- Daniel J. Rice

WITHIN THESE WOODS: A collection of Northwoods
nature essays with original illustrations by the author (2015)
- Timothy Goodwin

RELENTLESS: A Striker Mystery Novel (2015)
- Marcus Bruning & Jen Wright

ECOLOGICAL IDENTITY: Finding Your Place in a Biological
World (2016)
- Timothy Goodwin

TEACHERS IN THE FOREST: Essays from the last wilderness
in Mississippi Headwaters country (2016)
- Barry Babcock

ROAD TO PONEMAH: The Teachings of Larry Stillday (2016)
- Michael Meuers

AWAKE IN THE WORLD: A Riverfeet Press Anthology (2017)
-Various Authors